Frédérique Guéret

Stars and Flowers
Window Transparencies

Frédérique Guéret

Stars and Flowers Window Transparencies

Rudolf Steiner College Press

Dedicated to the magic light
of the Pyrenees and the Béarn
that filled my childhood days
with an unforgettable sense of beauty. . .

This publication has been made possible by a grant from the Waldorf Curriculum Fund.

ISBN 0-945803-76-1

Translator: Astrid Schmitt-Stegmann

The original edition in German (ISBN 3-7725-2223-8) was published in 2002 by Verlag Freies Geistesleben & Urachhaus GmbH

Photos: Wolpert & Strehle, Stuttgart
Illustrations: Frédérique Guéret

Book orders may be made through
Rudolf Steiner College Bookstore:
Tel. 916-961-8729, FAX 916-961-3032.
Catalog and online orders: www.steinercollege.edu.
Questions or comments, E-mail:
bookstore@steinercollege.edu.

Rudolf Steiner College Press
9200 Fair Oaks Boulevard
Fair Oaks, CA 95628, U.S.A.

Contents

Foreword

Window transparencies made of tissue paper are delicate sunlight creations. Their harmonious forms and the delightful play of color are only revealed by the light. Their colorful rays are like the magical facets of a prism when the light passes through. They always create a poetic mood. On the window these transparencies attract our gaze and take us on a journey of discovery, tracing the changing structures. Over and over a star or crystal, a rosette or blossom, call forth our amazement.

These stylized creations are not only a feast for the eyes but also an enrichment for other senses. Simply folding the light, supple paper brings much joy. Fingertip sensitivity is pleasantly enlivened as the lustrous tissue paper glides softly between the fingers. This activity alone awakens agility and develops a sense for form. You will spend many beautiful quiet moments engaged in this folding, filled with inner expectation of the completion of each precious shape.

Let yourself be guided by the detailed step by step instructions. You will discover, in spite of the seemingly complicated drawings, how stimulating this folding art can be. The visual movement from form to form becomes especially fascinating. Each form hides an inner logic that leads through transformations to a harmonious whole. This playful geometry of folding activates our thinking.

My wish for this book was to create new transparencies by a special method that would bring forth a variety of light effects. There was also the wish to develop a dynamic of forms in which the rotating movements could be partially unfolded to create a three-dimensionality. Some transparencies form a series that can be developed further. In this way, unexpected variables arise that give wings to our imagination.

Finally, through experimentation with colors, the artistic possibilities are further expanded.
May these transparencies be not only decorative images for the darker time of the year, but also a stimulation for the moods of celebration in other seasons.

Frédérique Guéret

Materials

paper	tissue paper of various colors (German "silk paper") See pages 10 and 12 for adaptations to different paper sizes.
construction board	a light-colored, strong piece of cardboard as a work surface
plastic sheet	a transparent plastic film for assembly of the rays
glue	transparent-drying crafts glue
bamboo stick	a thin skewer or other fine-pointed instrument for accurate application of the glue
adhesive tape	clear one-sided tape (1/2 inch wide) for attaching the transparency to a window
scissors	for cutting triangular pieces
ruler	only for checking equal sizes or spacings
pointed knife	for separating layers and smoothing the fine folds

For shading the color of the paper:

watercolors	(Yellow to red tones work best.) middle-sized paintbrush small sponge hairdryer

Symbols used in this book

*		very simple folding pattern
**		simple folding pattern; needs more attention
***		simple folding pattern; more difficult assembly
****		requires more dexterity
*****		unusual folding pattern; more complex assembly
(C)	=	center; glue point for assembly
(P)	=	outer point of ray
⊙	=	glue point
	=	glue point between foundation and first layer of paper
—	=	glue line
•	=	important orientation point and glue point between two pieces for more challenging assembly
	=	direction of folding process
	=	fold and reopen (preparatory fold for a support line)
	=	turn the piece over to work on the other side
⇛	=	pull out fold for special light effect
	=	crease with back of knife
	=	separate with knife

Enlivening the Paper

A good choice of color is important for making the pattern elements visible. Light orange, light pink, light blue, or light green bring out the contrasts between light and darkness very well. More intense colors seem super-saturated or flat, even when the form is shaped exactly. This is especially true with the red-blue or violet tones. You experience immediately that the color needs to be enlivened. The color can be lightened simply by removing some of the color from the paper before you cut it. Place your paper flat on a tile floor and try the following:

> If you want a subtle bead-like effect, take a wet brush (not too wet!) and sprinkle the paper here and there (as for Star Blossoms, p. 40).
>
> To make larger beads or spots, sprinkle the paper lightly by shaking the brush more forcefully (as in Light and Airy, p. 29).
>
> You can create a cloudy effect with a small, damp sponge (as in Ice Flower, p. 46).

Immediately after these improvisations, dry the paper with a hair dryer. Be sure to wipe the floor with clear water to avoid staining it with the colors from the paper.

If your aim is to create a step by step increase of yellow to orange tones (as in Warmth in Motion, p. 50), simply stack two or three papers, beginning with yellow and moving to stronger warm tones. Then use the sprinkling or sponging technique described above.

A further decorative enrichment can be achieved by adding a delicate tint to the paper with water colors. Do you want to warm a pale yellow? Or do you want to bring out a mysterious quality in the middle of a white transparency? There are no limits to a creative imagination! Dip the lightly dampened sponge into a dish of watercolor and dab the stacked papers in the exact places that you want to emphasize. You may want to use more than one color (as in Glowing Strength, p. 21).

In all these procedures, the paper will slightly wrinkle and will contract a little. After quick drying with the hair dryer, flatten out the paper with your hands when making the first fold so that it is as smooth as possible. When you have had sufficient practice in handling the paper in its original condition, it will be easier for you to work with slight irregularities created by these variations. The diameter of the pattern made with altered paper will naturally be slightly smaller than with paper in its original condition.

Cutting the Tissue Paper

The standard size of European tissue paper is 50 cm x 70 cm (19.7" x 27.6"). This size can be replicated by using 20" x 30" paper and shortening the 30" length by 2.4". Once this is done, no further measuring with a ruler is necessary. Just divide the paper according to the diagrams on pages 11–13. The measurements given in the instructions serve only as a guideline. Adaptations for other paper sizes are on page 12.

When you have chosen a color for your transparency, first fold the whole sheet in half—or into four parts if you need a quarter sheet. Before you cut the paper, check that the edges are alligned exactly; crease the paper carefully and slit the fold with a knife. Continue to fold and cut according to the size of square desired.

The basic shape of paper and number of pieces you need are listed at the beginning of each set of instructions. The shapes are shown by these symbols:

You also have the choice of working from two to four different sizes.

If you are a beginner in the art of folding, start with the easy transparencies (* or **) and select a large size format.

Square Cuts

In this book you will usually create transparencies that are based on a square. Diagonals and centered folds are starting points for many varied shapes. You do not need a protractor. First fold and cut a half or quarter sheet following drawings I and II. You will only need to cut the resulting large square into four or sixteen parts (Cuts 1–5).

Triangular Cuts

You make triangles from the squares by folding and cutting along the diagonal (drawing III). Use scissors for the beginning and end of the cut.

Rectangular Cuts

Rectangular papers are the leftovers from several square cuts (Cuts 6 & 7). Long strips (Cuts 8 & 9) are for the multifoliate Rose pattern only.

Diagrams for Formats

For each set of cuts, there are two drawings: The upper drawing shows the whole sheet of paper. The lower one with a shaded area shows the section you will use. The measurements are not needed for construction of the star; they are given only so you can check the steps as you go along. The color of the drawings makes it easy to identify the basic shapes:

Basic instructions for cutting pieces of different sizes are on page 11. The required sizes are given at the beginning of the instructions for each pattern.

Cutting the Paper

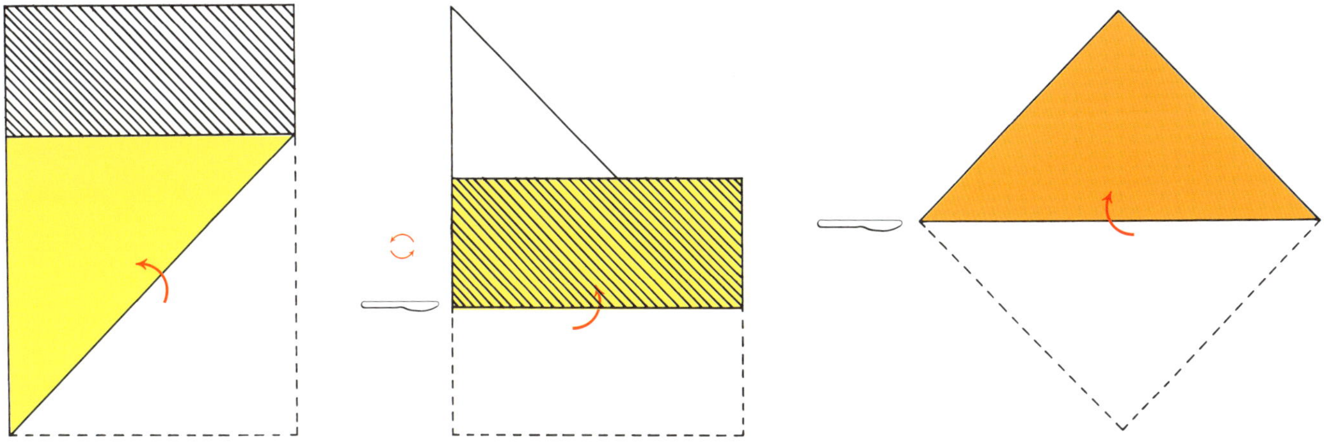

Diagrams for Formats

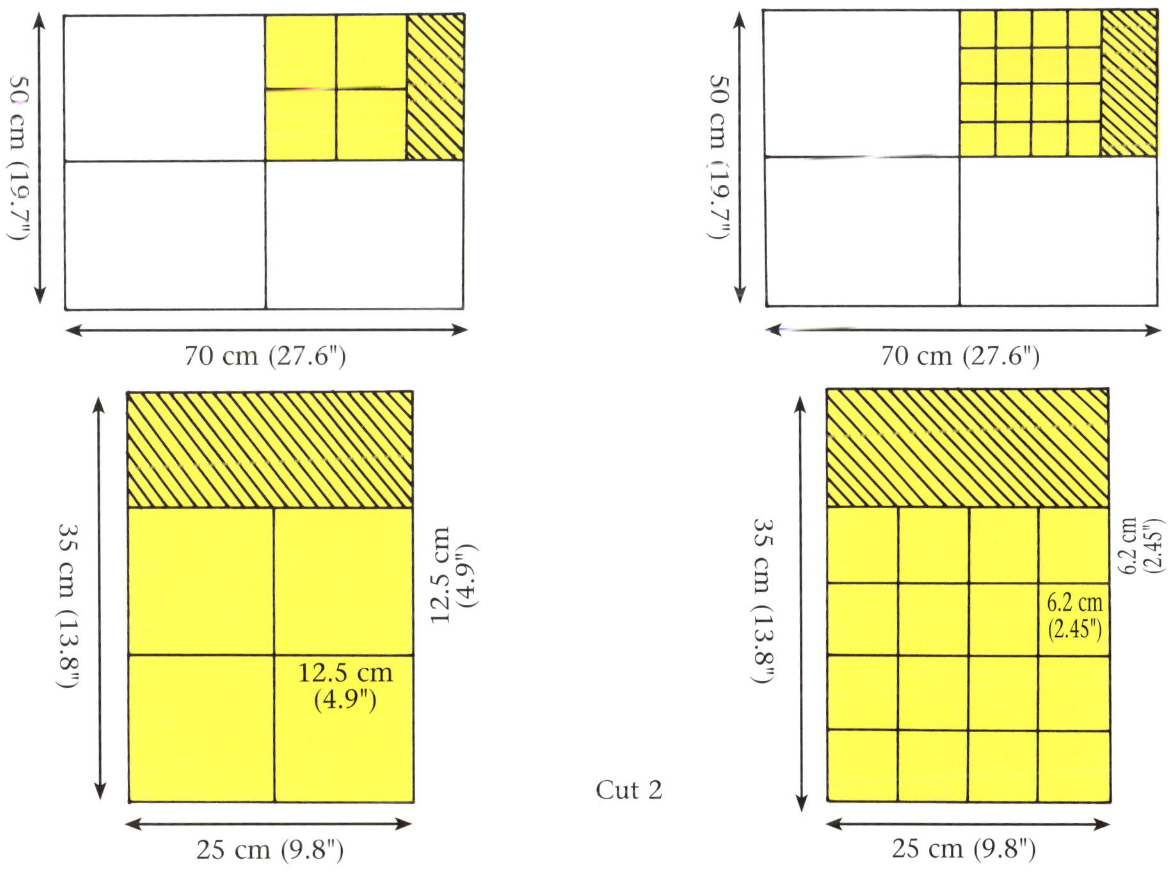

Cut 1

Cut 2

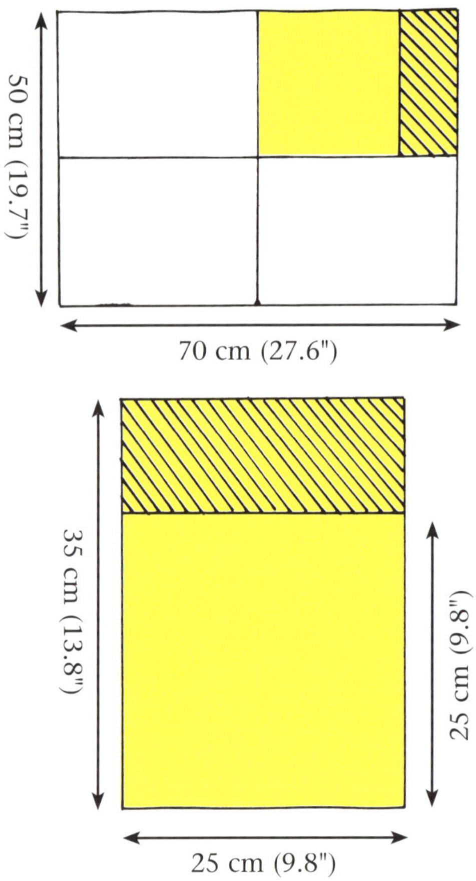

Cut 3

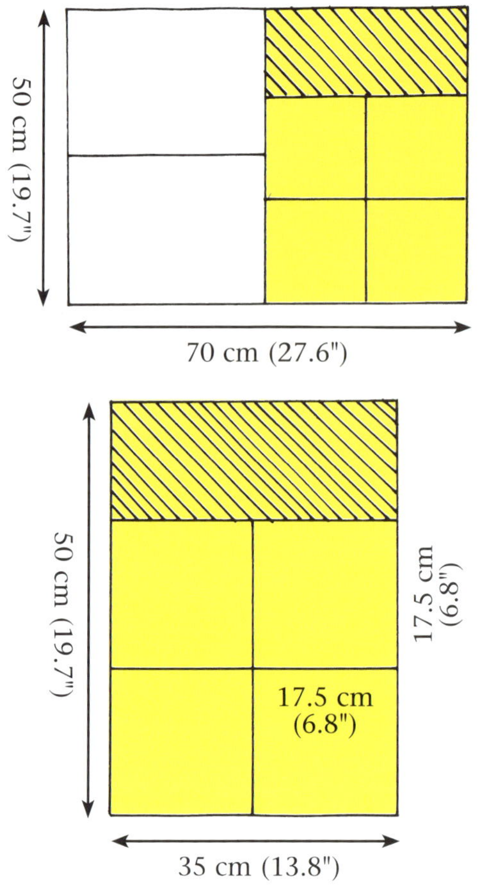

Cut 4

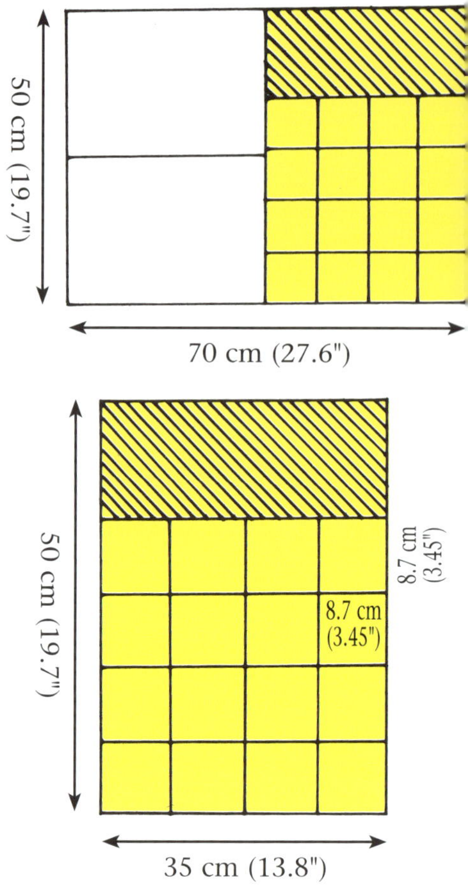

Cut 5

Adapting instructions to different paper sizes

Cut 20" x 30" paper down to match European size as shown on page 10. The Satin Wrap Company produces this size paper in many beautiful shades (see www.satinwrap.com). European silk paper (50 cm x 70 cm) may be ordered from Wendt & Wendt in Hamburg, Germany (see www.wendtundwendt.de).

Alternately, 20" x 26" (50.8 cm x 66 cm) tissue paper may be used for all except Cuts 6 and 7 (for Patterns 23 and 24). The results will be slightly smaller or larger than the diameters given in the instructions.

Patterns 23 and 24 may be made by cutting squares to match the sizes of Cuts 6 and 7 on page 13.

Craft tissue 20" x 20" (50.8 cm x 50.8 cm) sold in many craft shops may be used for Cuts 1, 2 , and 3 and will produce figures larger than the diameter given in the instructions. For other cuts, the paper needs to be measured and cut according to the dimensions given on pages 12 and 13.

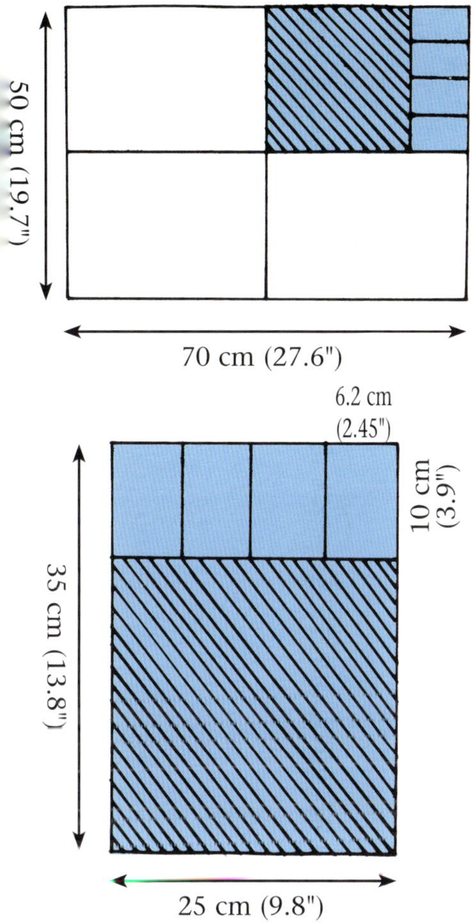

Cut 6

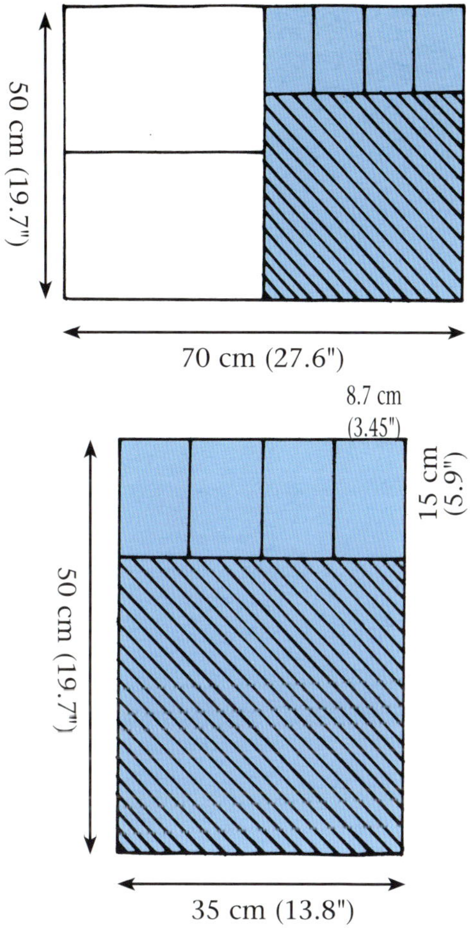

Cut 7

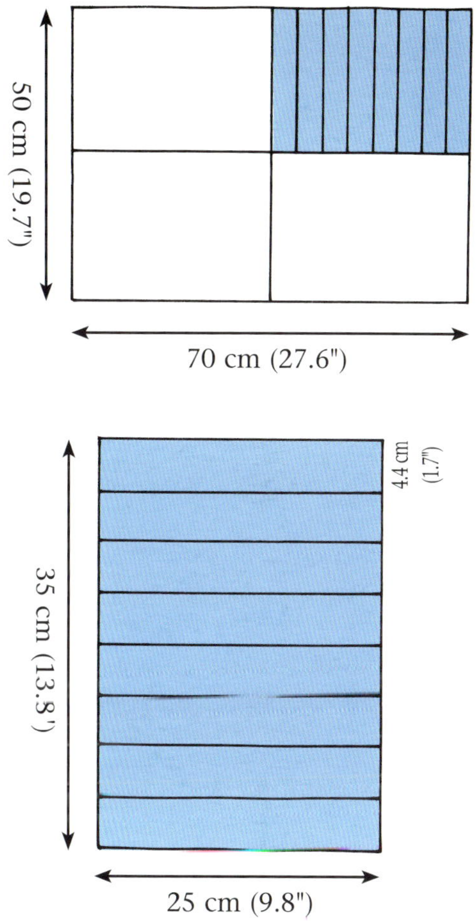

Cut 8

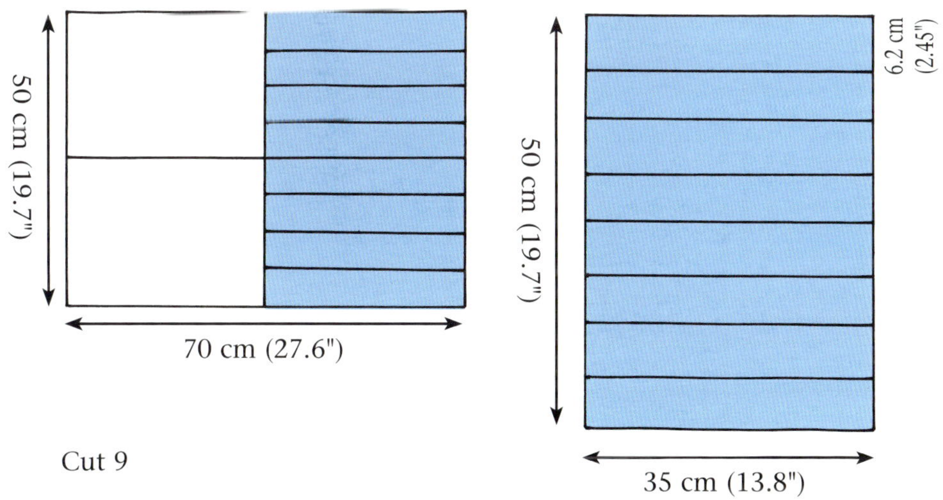

Cut 9

Assembly:

From the segment to the whole

When all the segments have been folded, you have the thrilling moment when you see what the final form will look like. First, place a plastic sheet on cardboard as a work surface. Place the segments one beside the other working clockwise. The folded sides of the segments face upward.

1.

Figures with 8 rays

Place the first segment flat with the center (C) oriented toward you. Working clockwise, lay the second segment on top of the first one so that the left edge of the second lies along the midline of the first. With the bamboo stick, apply a tiny dab of glue to the underside of the second segment at the center (C). Join the two segments with the center points overlapping exactly. Then join the segments with a tiny bit of glue along the line where the left edge of the second piece meets the midline of the first (Picture 1).

Attach each succeeding piece in the same way (Picture 2).

2.

When you have glued the 8th segment, lift the left edge of the first segment over the top of the 8th (or slide the 8th below it) in order to attach this edge to the midline of the 8th segment (Picture 3).

3.

Carefully turn the transparency over and secure all the rays as needed with tiny dabs or lines of glue (Picture 4). Before admiring your transparency in the light, see the instructions for fastening the transparency to a window on page 17.

4.

Figures with five and six rays

The assembly principle is the same. However, since segments for a 5- or 6-pointed figure will not meet at the midlines, you will need to use a diagram to arrange the spacing. Make an enlarged photocopy of the 5- and 6-pointed patterns below. Lengthen the given lines with a red pencil. Place the diagram under the plastic sheet. Place the midline of your folded segments along these red lines as you assemble the pattern. In this manner you will be able to construct a five-pointed star or a snow crystal without problems.

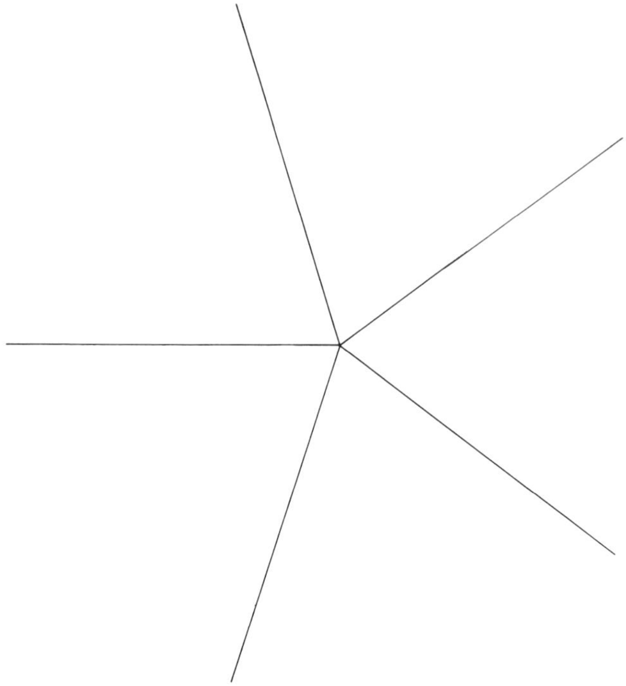

Assembly template for five-ray patterns

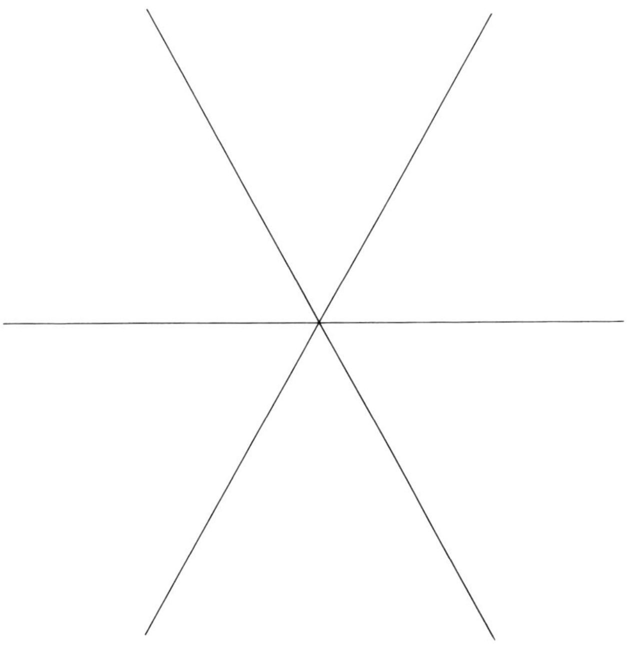

Assembly template for six-ray patterns

Figures with four, nine, ten, eleven, and fourteen rays

Midlines do not help us with assembly of these stars. We need to find a new orientation for each new figure. Step-by-step drawings are included for each pattern indicating a key starting point (•) or edge to use as the glue point. This orientation and glue point is the hidden key to the whole construction.

Fastening the Transparency to a Window

The details of the patterns become completely visible only when they are in a window. Light shining through them brings out the beauty of the colors and shapes. They show up best when you attach the smooth underside to the glass. With three-dimensional forms, this is the only way since the loose folds are on the front side of the transparencies.

Attach short pieces of adhesive tape to the underside of the tip of every second or third ray, in places where the paper is not too thin. These will be reinforced points where separate tiny rolls of tapes can stick the transparency to a window without tearing the fragile paper. These little rolls are very practical and can be used often, so you can change the position of your transparencies as often as you like. In this way you can protect the delicate paper of your favorites and enjoy them for years.

The colors tend to fade somewhat after a few months, but this creates an autumn-like quality that also has its charm.

Transparencies reveal different nuances as the quality of the light changes from morning to evening. Even at night in the glow of street lights, the transparencies continue to diffuse their mysterious presence.

Folding Your First Transparency

1. Starglow *

figure with 8 rays
diameter:
35 cm (13.8") Cut 4
25 cm (9.8") Cut 1

This strongly structured star displays a harmonious distribution of light and shadow. Loose folds on the short outer rays as well as on the inner rosette highten this effect.

Take 8 squares, following either cut 4 or cut 1. Fold the two middle lines according to the small drawing above.

1.–3. Follow the steps of the folding process indicated in the drawings. Consider the middle lines and diagonals as "main arteries" on which the other folds are based.

The broken lines in the drawing always show the previous fold line. Arrows and shading show the folding steps.

< *A light orange shows the structure of lines effectively.*

1.

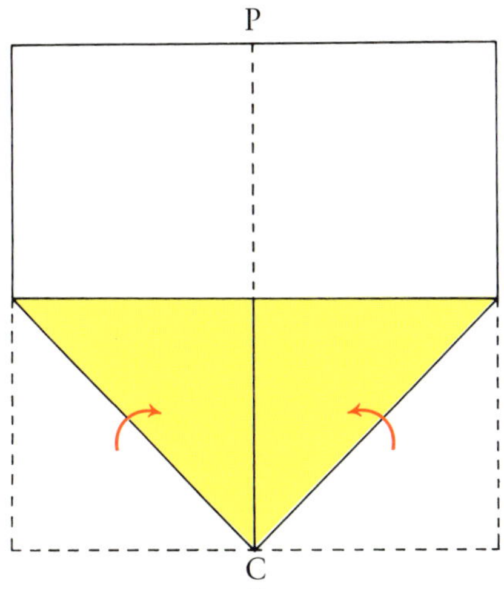

2.

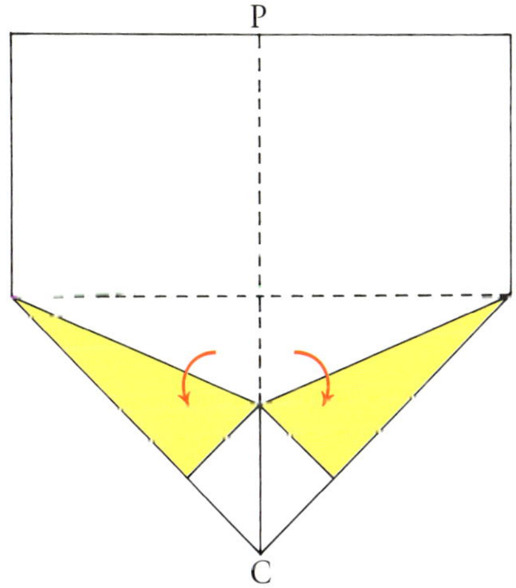

3.

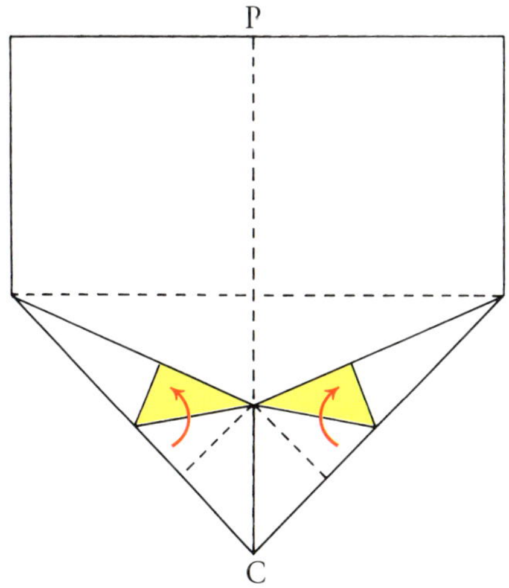

This star was tinted lightly with yellow at the center and tips. In contrast to the basic vanilla yellow color, a delicate light ring appears between the center and periphery.

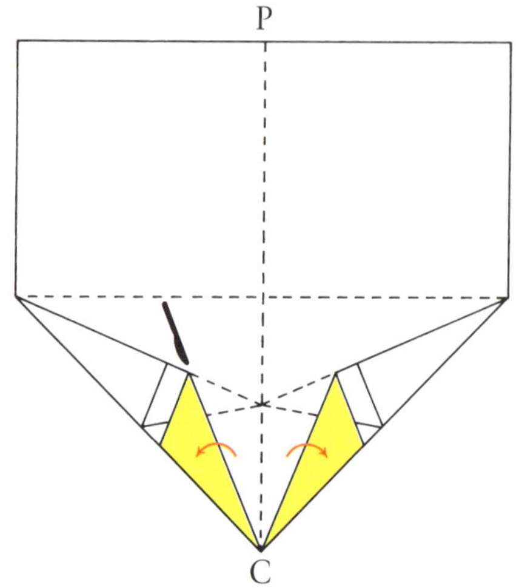

4.

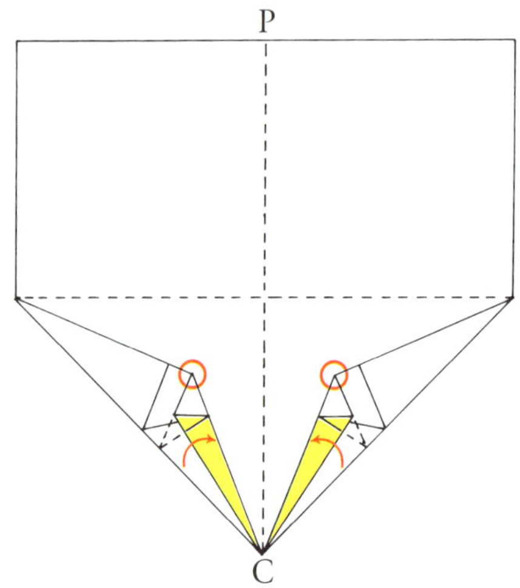

5.

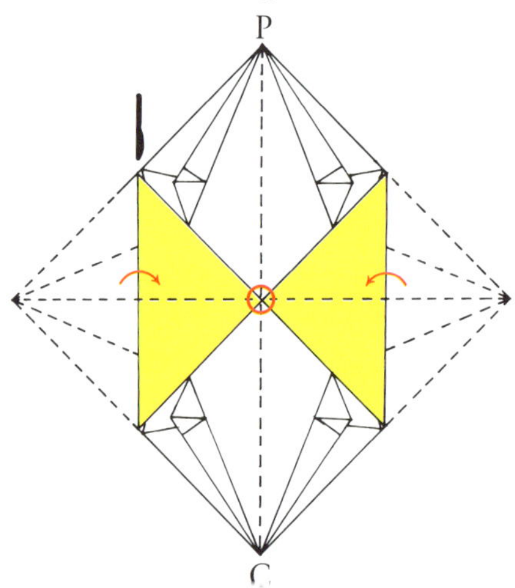

6.

4. In order to fold with precision, use the dull side of a knife blade as a tool. While folding, let it glide slowly between the two layers of paper, thus avoiding slippage of the lower layer.

5. **Do not forget the two glue points.** *After folding the center point (C), you will fold the point (P).*

6. Fold the side wings to the center; crease the folds with the knife and lightly glue the wing points to the midpoint.

The 8 segments are now folded, each one already presenting a harmonious form.

Now begins the assembly of the rays, a very thrilling moment every time (see directions for figures with 8 rays on page 14). The inner rosette has alternating loose and fastened folds. The outer points were not glued, giving this form a soft lightness.

By removing some of the color from the tissue paper before folding, the bright orange was toned down to make it more luminous.

2. *Glowing Strength* **

figure with 8 rays
diameter:
35 cm (13.8") Cut 4
25 cm (9.8") Cut 1

The strength of the first star's rays is changed to a quieter glowing warmth by continuing the folding process. Open vertically folded triangles encircle the inner rosette, creating more color contrast between the center and the outer points.

Begin by folding the rays as for steps 1–6 of Starglow, but *without gluing the side wings to the center.*

1. Glue points are indicated in the (P) area only.

2. Pull the inner angles slightly towards the middle. Creasing with the dull side of the knife blade is absolutely essential here! Now glue the middle.

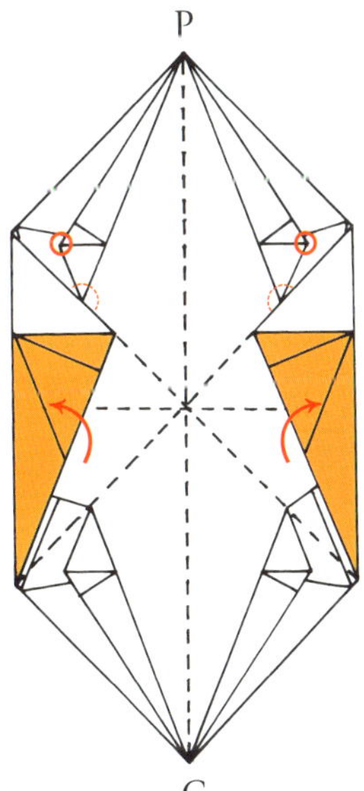

1.

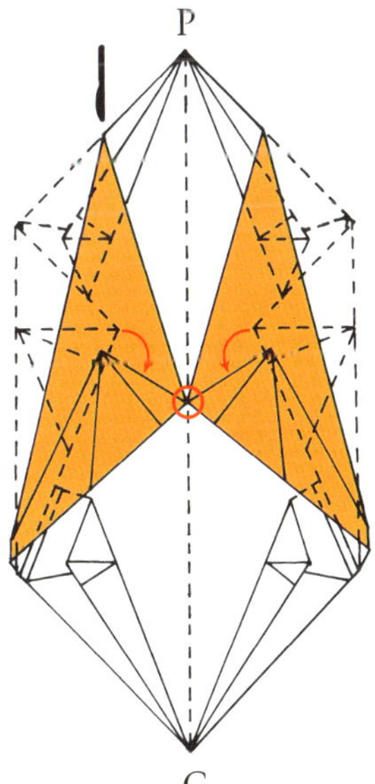

2.

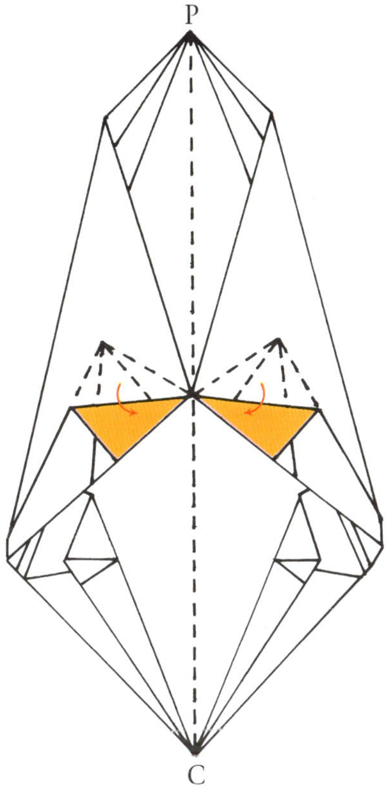

3.

3. Fold these corners firmly and leave them unglued and open at a right angle.

Assemble as before. Note, however, that the last fold stays vertical; do not add it into the assembly. On the window, you can lift these open folds slightly so that they form a loose center for a three-dimensional effect.

< *In this transparency, a special effect is created by using yellow-orange and pink watercolors on white paper.*

3. Sun Blossoms ***

figure with 9 rays
diameter:
33 cm (13") Cut 4
23 cm (9") Cut 1
16.5 cm (6.5") Cut 5

Depending on the choice of color, these sun blossoms give us spring or autumn greetings. In the center, a rhythmic circle of delicate triangles appears. Figures with nine rays are also uncommon.

Take 9 squares in one of the sizes listed above. This time we will use diagonals as our "main arteries."

1–2. Make the initial fold lines. The next fold will end in a sharp point. *The upper half of the segment needs to be formed with exactness and care.*

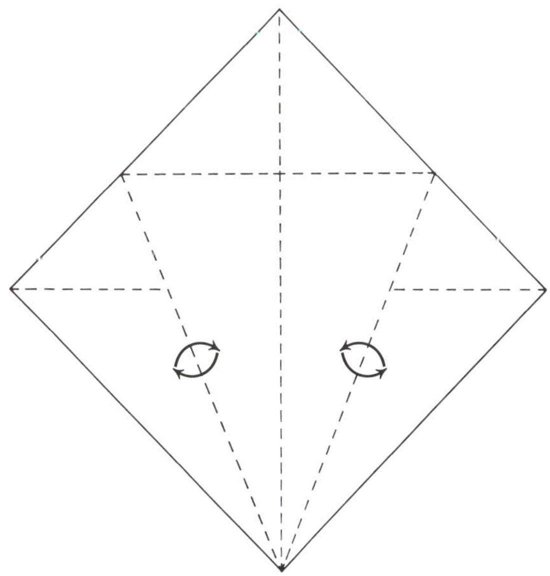

1.

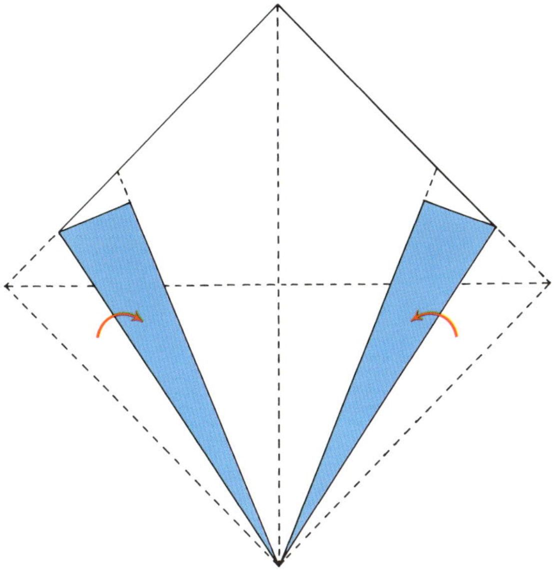

2.

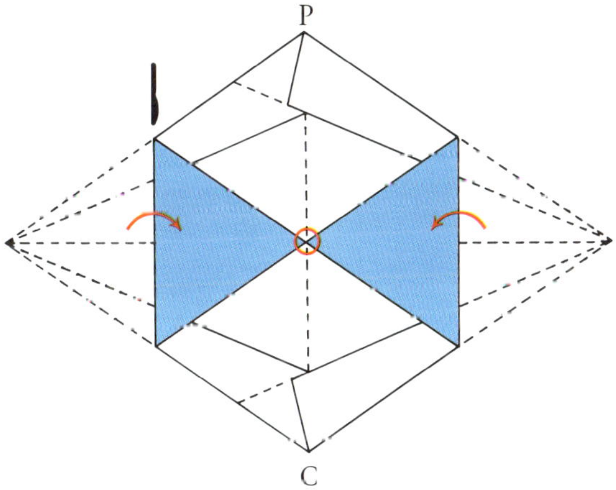

3.

3. The angle with the inner edge oriented to the left will become the final center (C). Close the side wings, creasing with the knife, and glue them to the center point.

4–7. Continue folding according to the diagrams.

< *After folding the large straw-yellow transparency, we tinted the edges of the rays with light blue watercolor felt pen, making them appear light green, harmonizing with the fresh spring green of the smaller star.*

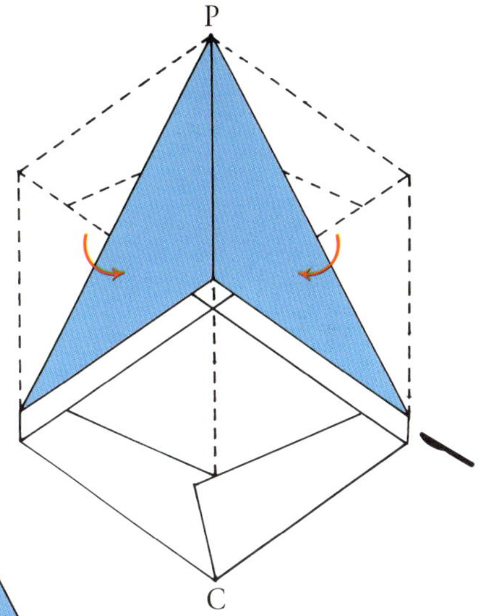

4.

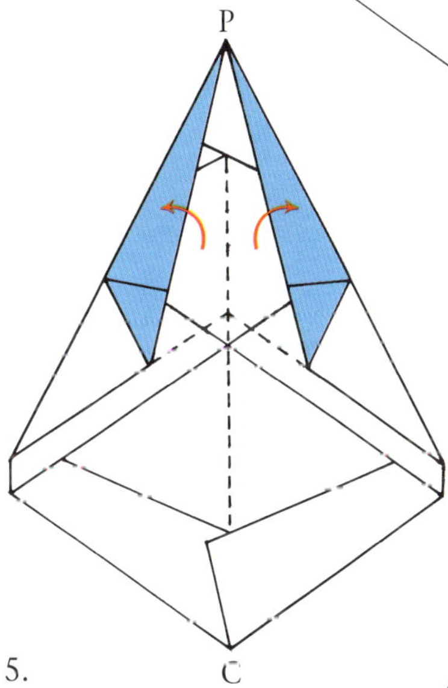

5.

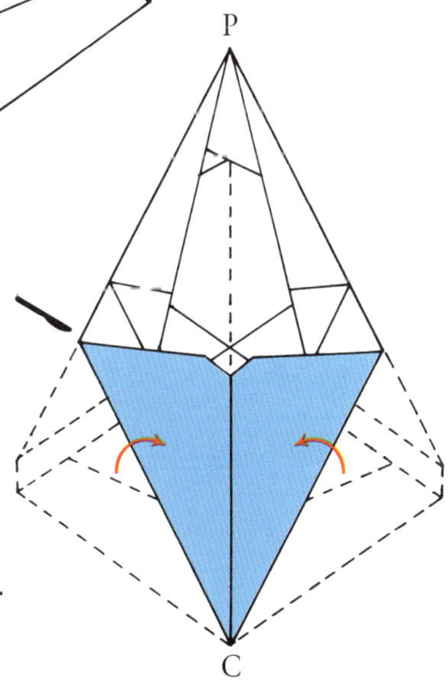

6.

7. 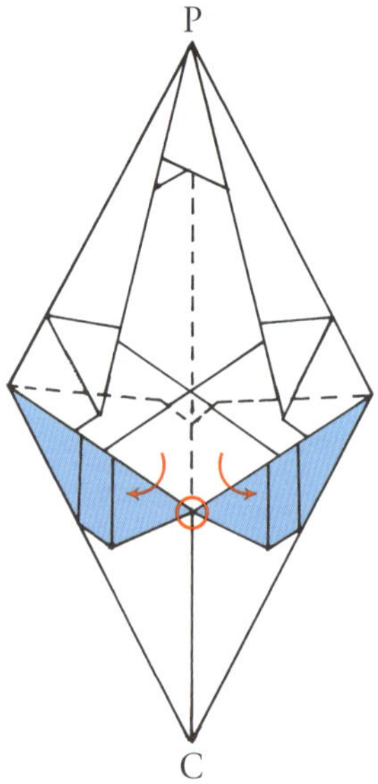

8. To assemble the 9 rays (see instructions, p. 16), locate the orientation point • near the right inner edge:

- for cut 4, the orientation point is 3/32" (1.5 mm) from the fold,
- for cut 1, the orientation point is 1/16" (1 mm) from the fold,
- for cut 5, the orientation point is exactly on the fold.

Start with only a few glue points so that you can correct the spacing slightly if need be. After assembling, glue the loose folds if you wish to emphasize the structure. If you leave them open, these Sun Blossoms will be light and airy.

All folds of the warm red transparency were glued, emphasizing the line structure. We added a beautiful brown tone to the middle-sized transparency and enlivened it with light yellow dots.

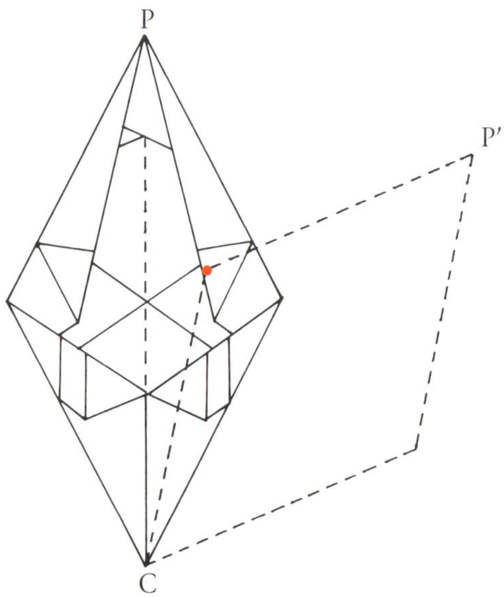

8.

4. *Star Crystal* ****

figure with 6 rays
diameter:
33 cm (13") Cut 4
23.5 cm (9.25") Cut 1
16.5 cm (6.5") Cut 5

This beautiful clear crystal is a metamorphosis of the previous transparency. We can still see the chain of triangles in the center; however, the final result has a completely new character. The light penetrates right to the calyx of the finely chiselled ice blossom, while the veiled ray points reflect tranquility toward the center.

Take 6 squares cut to dimensions of 4, 1 or 5 and follow steps 1–6 for Sun Blossoms (p. 23).

1. Pull the inner fold at (P) with the tip of the knife. This process is indicated by the symbol ⇛. Pull it out as you would pull out a loop and lay it to the left, smoothing it down flat, following the drawing. At (C) open both folds.

2. Now fold the (P) fold to the right. Fold (C) according to the drawing.

3. As above, pull out the second inner fold at (P) with the tip of the knife (⇛), then slowly pull out the whole folded section. Fold this over the inner edge to the left. What remains is a cone form which you lay flat. Place the top corner exactly along the midline. Use the tip of the knife to guide you. At (C) follow the same procedure.

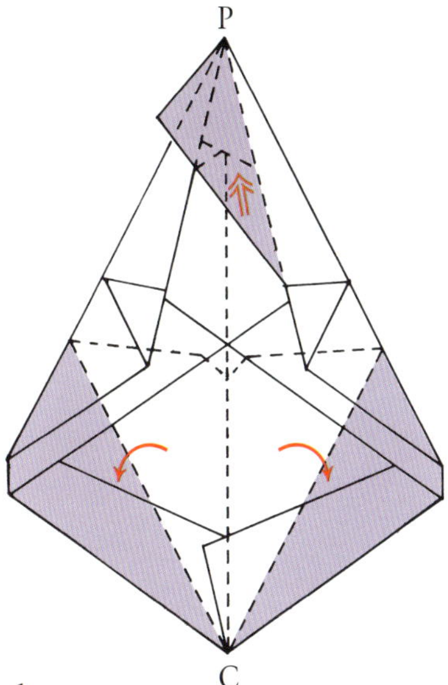

1.

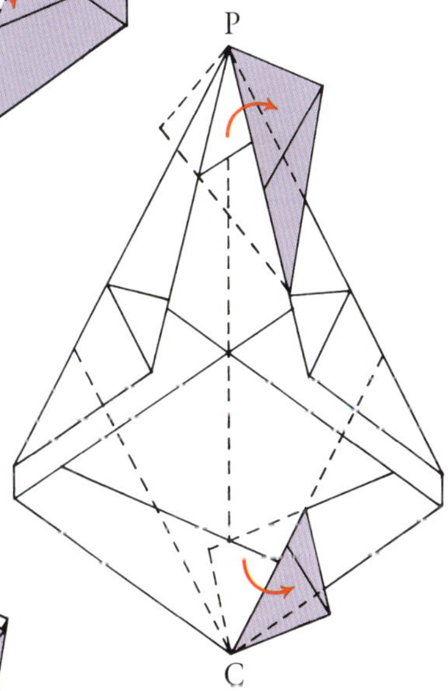

2.

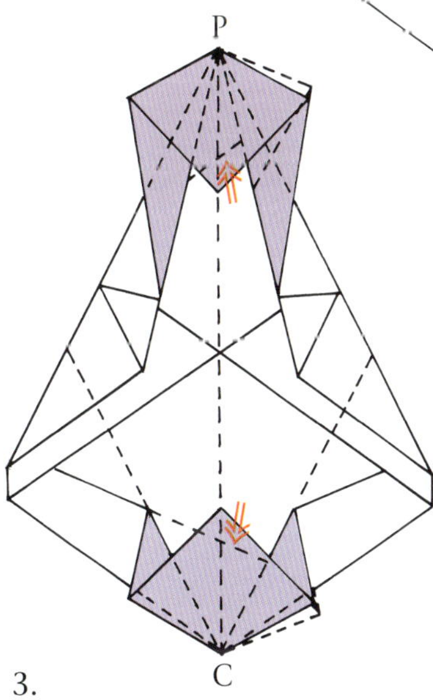

3.

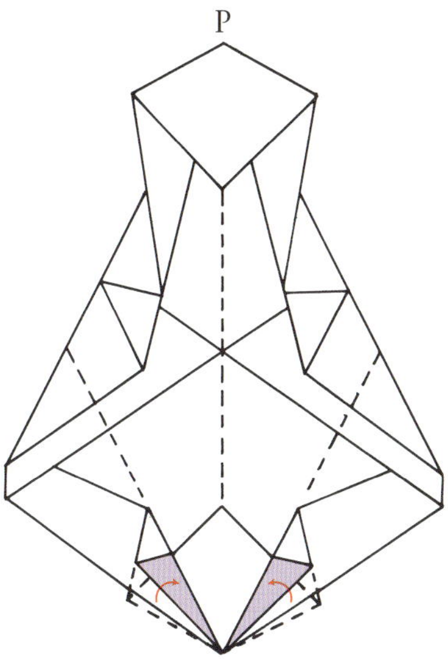

4.

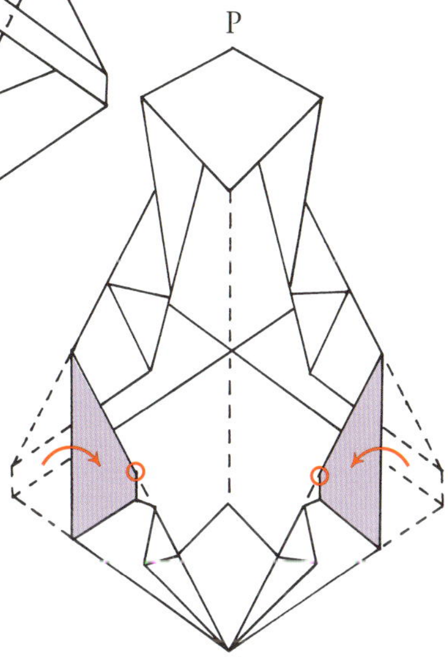

5.

4. Here (C) is further refined. Note that it needs to remain sharply pointed.

5. Fold and glue the side wings.

Assemble the 6 folded rays according to instructions on page 16.

You may want to pull out the unglued edges of the outer rays and the inner blossom slightly. You could do the same with the graceful loose tips.

< *The paper for the light pink crystal was lightly sprinkled with water drops.*

5. Light and Airy **

figure with 5 rays
diameter:
28 cm (11") Cut 4
21 cm (8.25") Cut 1
14.5 cm (5.7") Cut 5

These star blossoms seem to fall from heaven, light and airy. Loose inside folds underline this feeling of lightness.

Take 5 squares and fold the diagonal lines.

Some of the turquoise color of this star blossom was removed by dabbing the paper with a small sponge, giving a blended effect to this pattern.

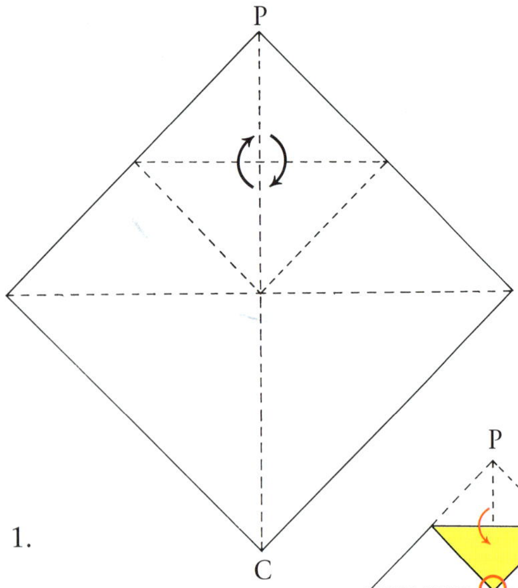

1.

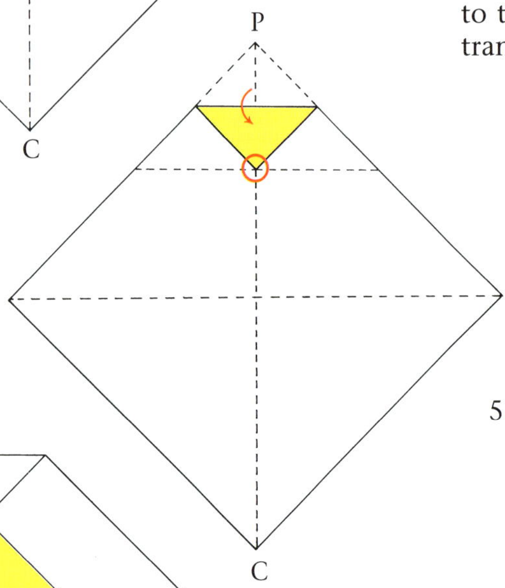

2.

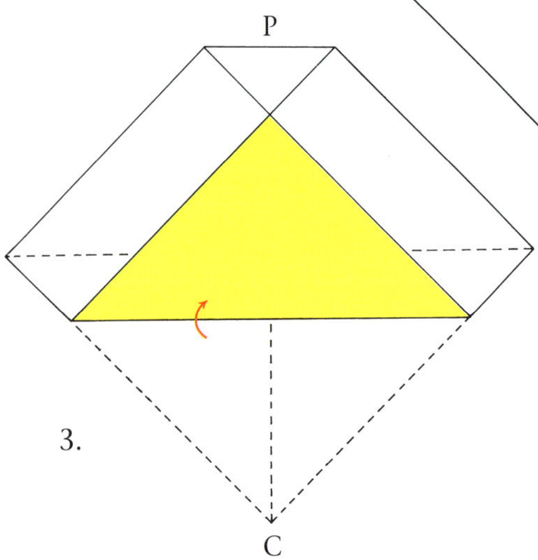

3.

1–3. Fold according to the steps indicated in the diagrams.

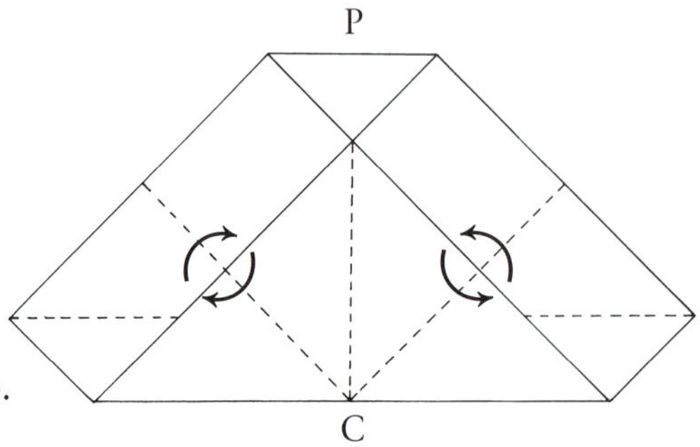

4.

4. Fold the side wings along the diagonal according to the diagram and open them out again, creating transverse support lines.

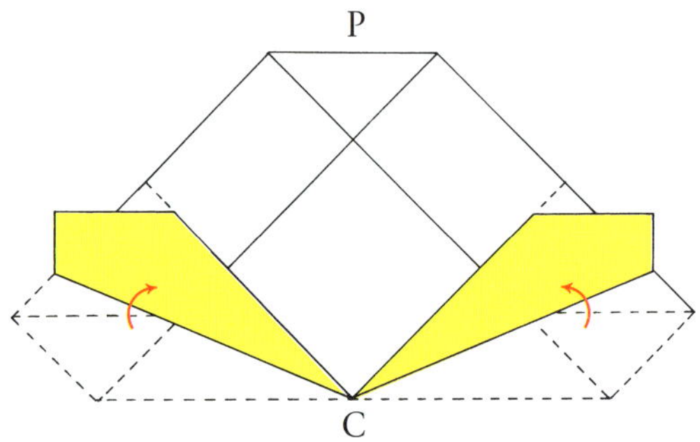

5.

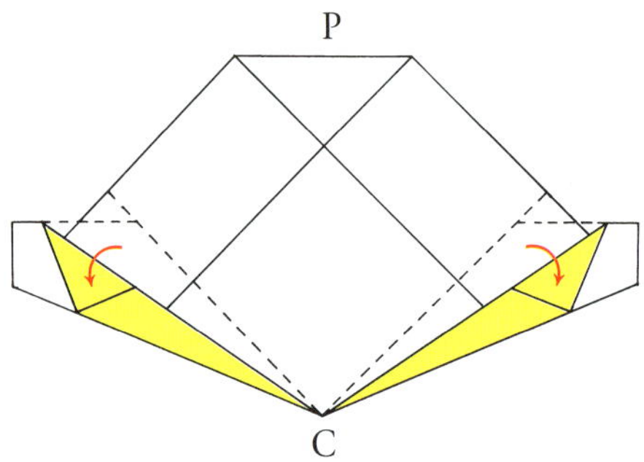

6.

5–7. Continue folding according to the diagrams. *Turn the segment over.*

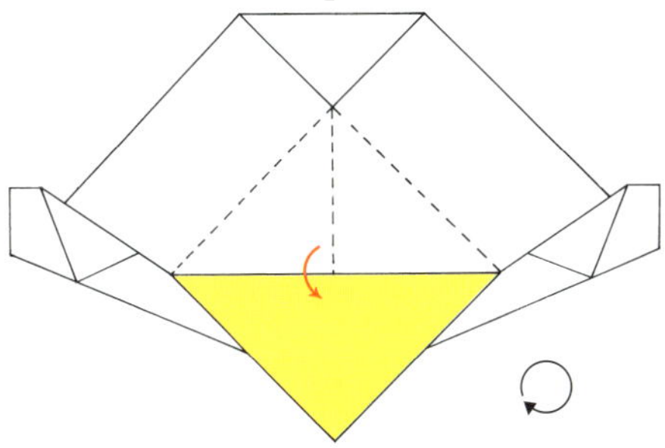

7.

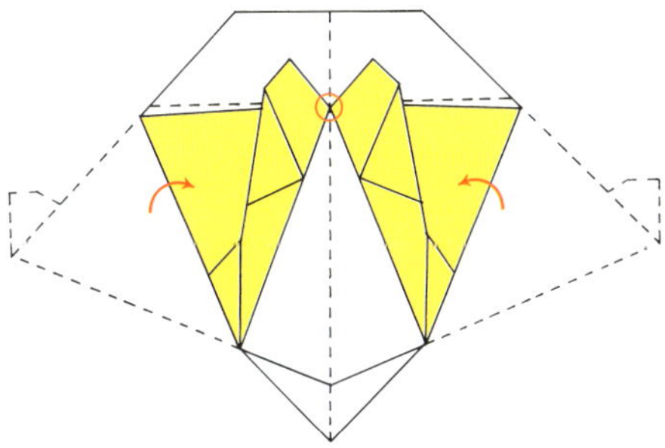

8.

8. Fold the wings back and fasten them at the midline with a dot of glue. This segment side with the unglued inner edges will be *the front side* of the finished transparency.

Assemble the star using the diagram for 5-ray patterns (see page 16). Since in this pattern the tips of the segments are glued to the midline, you must place your segments so that the midline corresponds to the diagram lines. Be very sparing with the glue, especially in the center (C) where the tissue paper is not folded.

Are these airy star blossoms or light blossom stars that waft like butterflies on the window?

Sprinkled with white dots, this little star blossom seems to want to dance. The paper for the light orange star was left as is, its blue complementary color sufficiently present in the background of the sky.

6. Sun Seal **

figure with 8 rays
diameter:
30.5 cm (12") Cut 1
21 cm (8.25") Cut 5
15.5 cm (6.1") Cut 2

This very effective transparency reminds us of an old custom when, at the time of the summer solstice, villagers lit wooden wheels and rolled them down the mountain on St. John's night.

This sun wheel is remarkable in that it displays an unusual center when the pattern is assembled.

Fold the diagonals for the 8 segments especially accurately.

First fold according to drawings 1 and 2 for Sun Blossoms, pages 23 and 25.

Then continue with diagrams 1 and 2 for Light and Airy, page 30.

1. Glue the two upper and lower points to the fold line.

2. Carefully unfold the side angles all the way down to the delicate covered points and slowly crease them flat.

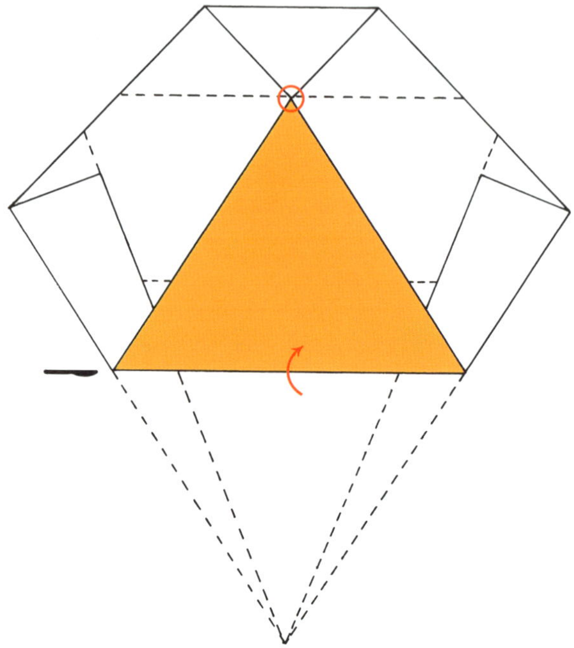

1.

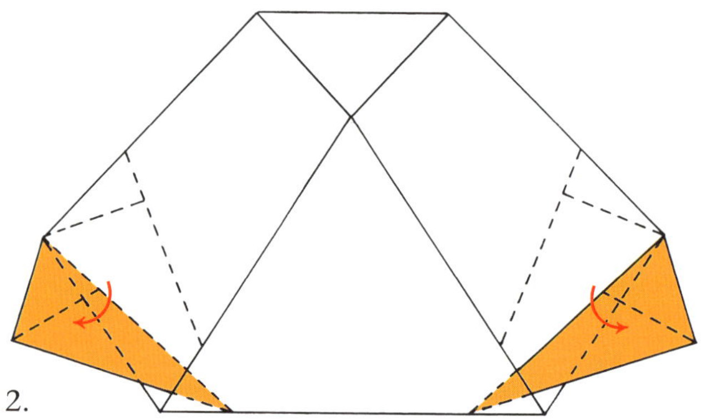

2.

For this Sun Seal a little of the red paper color was removed. >

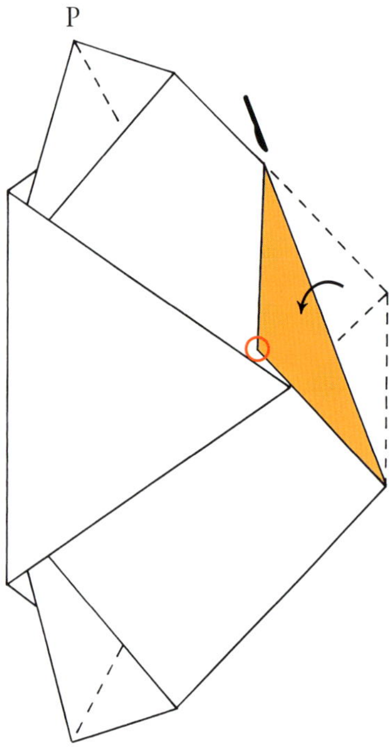

3.

3. Rotate the piece so that *the right corner becomes the center* (C). Fold, smooth, and glue the new right point according to the diagram.

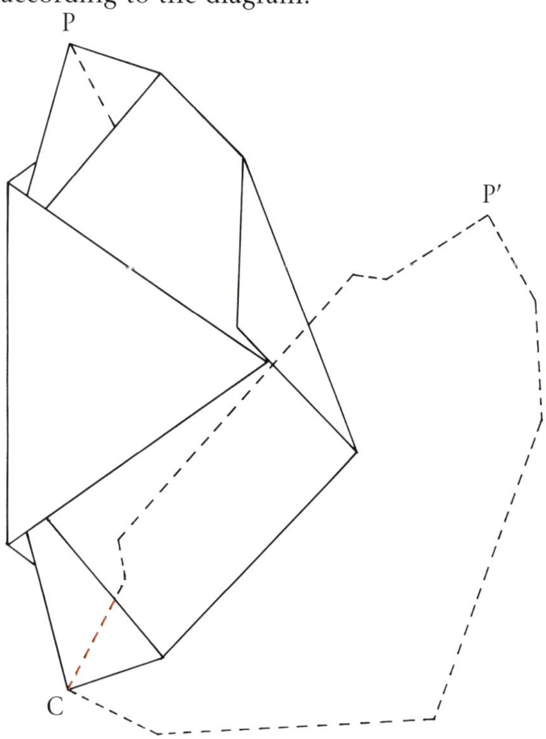

4.

To the orange Sun Seal with no color changes, we add a smaller one in which the basic color is enhanced with light orange dots.

4. Although point (C) is unusually placed, proceed assembling as for all eight-ray transparencies (see instructions, p. 14). The old diagonal at (C)—dotted in red—is the support line. Depending on transparency size and treatment of the paper, the left side of the second segment will meet more or less accurately the glued tip of the previous segment. Use very little glue on the (C) points as there are no folds there. With this transparency, there is no possibility for a three-dimensional look.

7. Fragile Ice Crystal ***

figure with 6 rays
diameter:
38 cm (15") Cut 1
27 cm (10.6") Cut 5

Before this snowflake melts away completely, it reveals its delicate filigreed structure. The winter fairy was at work again!

This crystal does not take long to make since half of the pattern is not folded.

Fold diagonals in 12 squares. Then establish the (C) point by folding according to drawings 1 and 2 of Light and Airy (p. 30).

1–3. Continue folding according to the drawings.

The rose-colored spots on this large, elegant snowflake are made before cutting the paper. Take 3 sheets of tissue paper (which will be cut into 12 squares) and sponge watercolor paint into the center of each, using a circular motion.

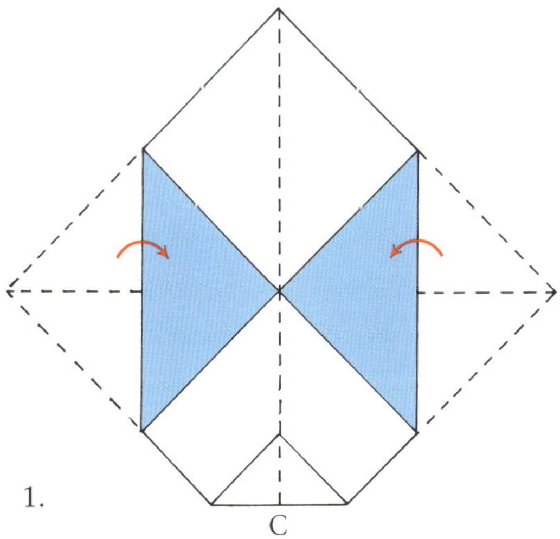

1.

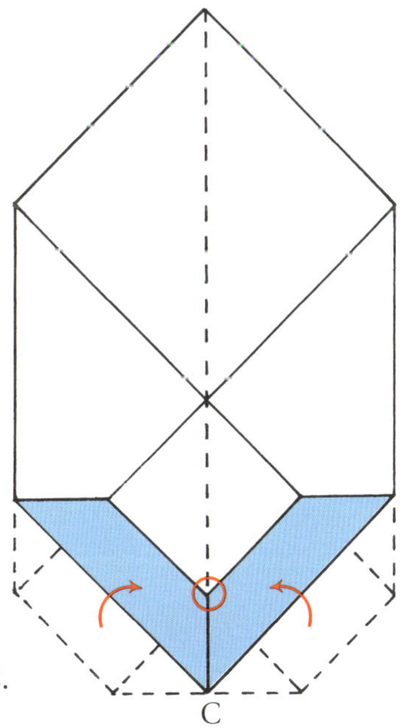

2.

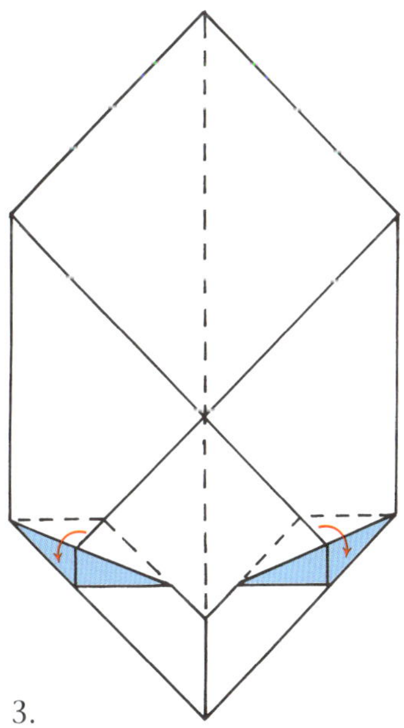

3.

The paper for the two-tone transparency was pretreated by making light blue spots on white paper and white sprinkles on blue paper. The fine marbled effect of the sky-blue crystal was made by leaching color from the paper with water drops.

4. Pull gently on the two middle loose angles so that the lower corners are free.

5. Fold side wings outward. To do this, hold down the freed triangle of the (C) side with your index finger as you bend the wing outward. Crease this fold exactly.

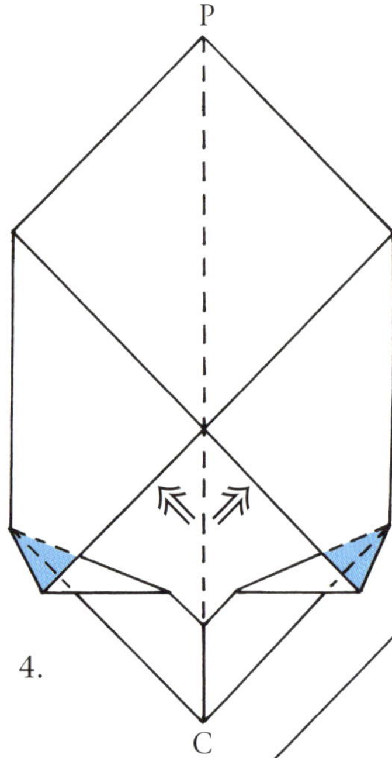

4.

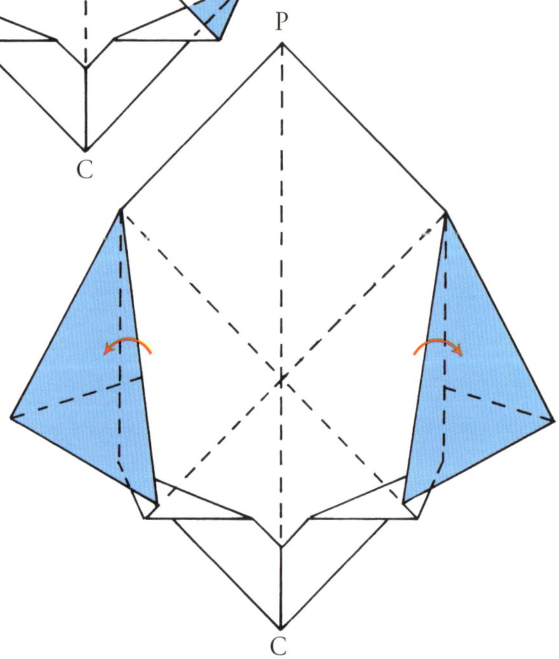

5.

6. Assemble 6 of the folded segments into a 6-rayed pattern (see page 16). Then glue the other 6 segments as in the diagram. It is important that the midline of each added segment is alligned exactly with the crossing point of each pair of the original segments. The folds can be fastened with long thin glue streaks. The lines of this 6-pointed crystal made with 12 parts stand out very clearly when the folds are glued down.

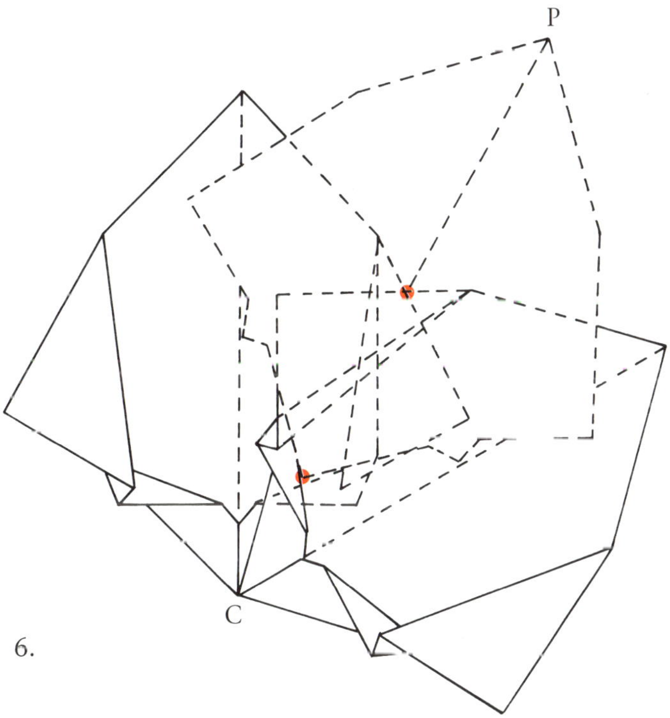

6.

The pink stars were each done in one unaltered color. >

8. Mood of the Fifth ****

figure with 5 rays
diameter:
32.5 cm (12.8") Cut 4
23 cm (9") Cut 1
16 cm (6.3") Cut 5

Five-part forms bring a feeling of calm and peace. Enfolded in its silky folds, a star dreams like a seed in the core of an apple.

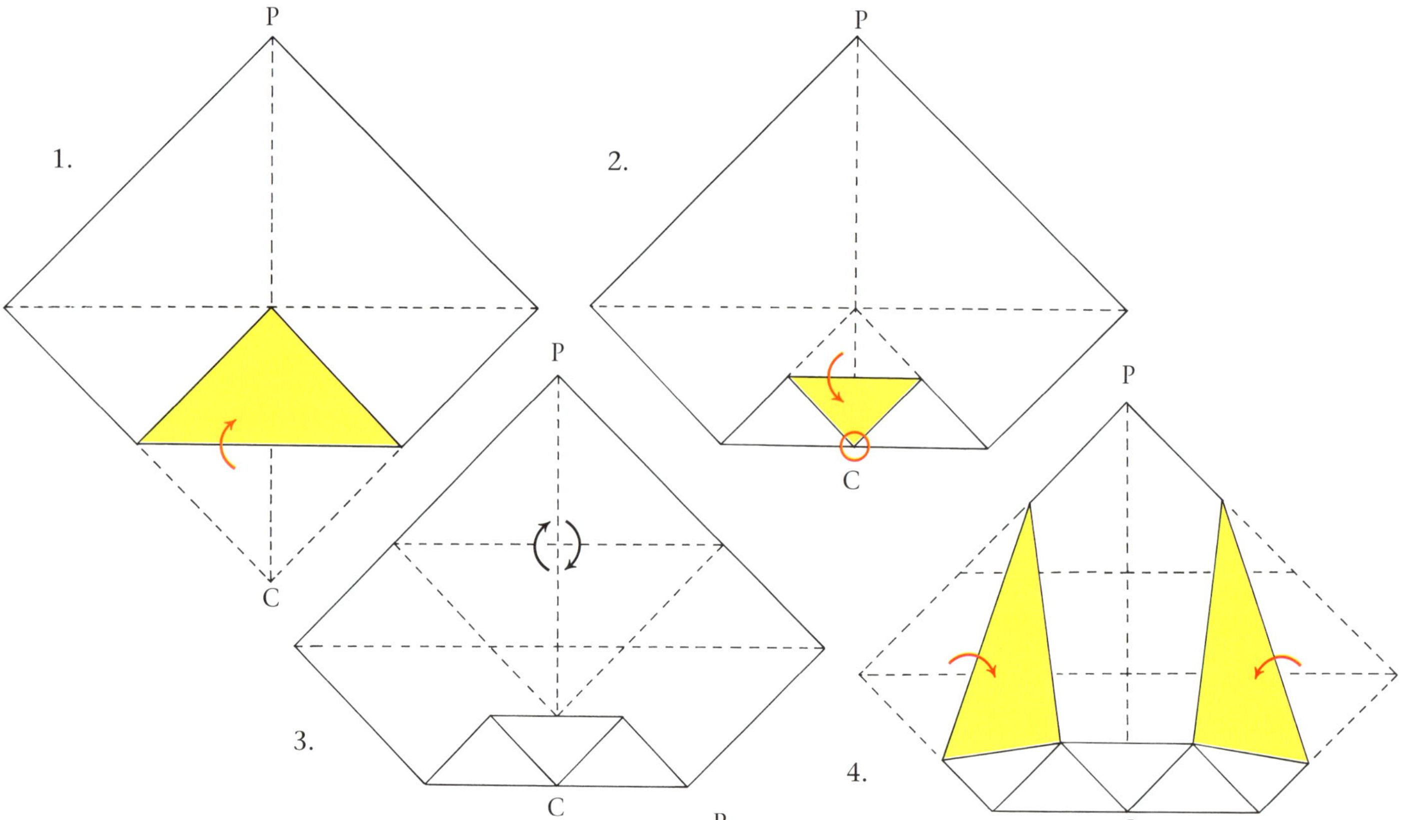

1–4. Fold diagonals in 5 squares. Continue folding according to the diagrams.

5. Fold the (P) point to the crossing point of the diagonal and the support line. Fold the side wing points back to their own edge folds.

6. Use the back of the knife to help with these delicate folds. Shape point (P). Mark the indicated glue points now.

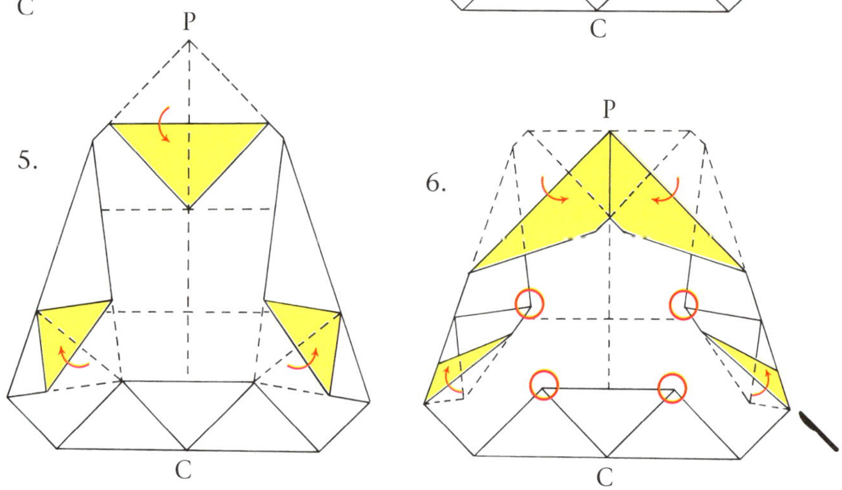

To prepare paper for this star, lay a sheet of lemon yellow paper on top of a sheet of lime green. Blend the colors together by swabbing with a damp sponge. >

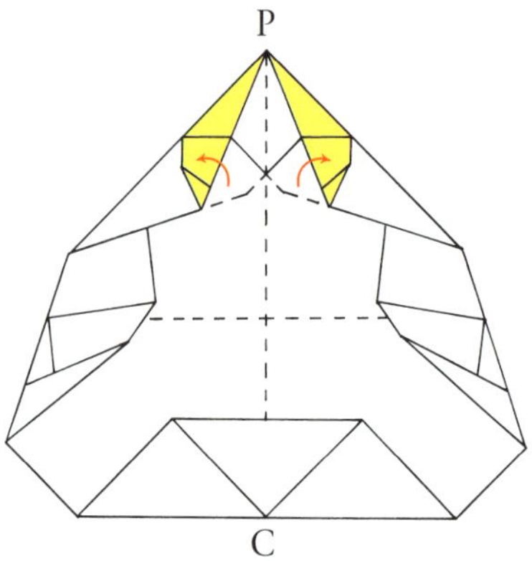

7.

7. Fold back the side points near (P).

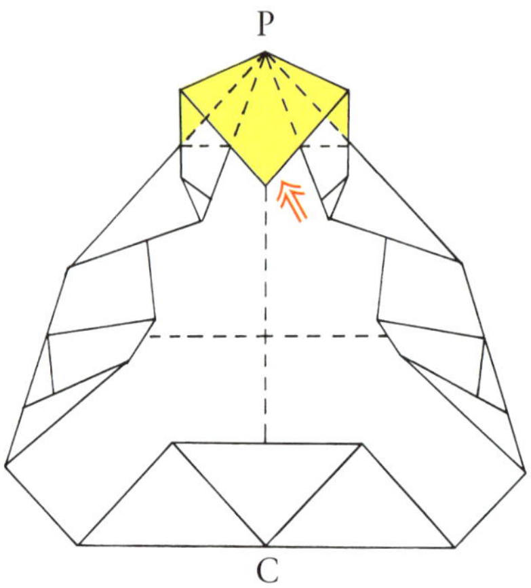

8.

8. Slowly pull out the loose inner angles at (P) then smooth these folds with your fingers.

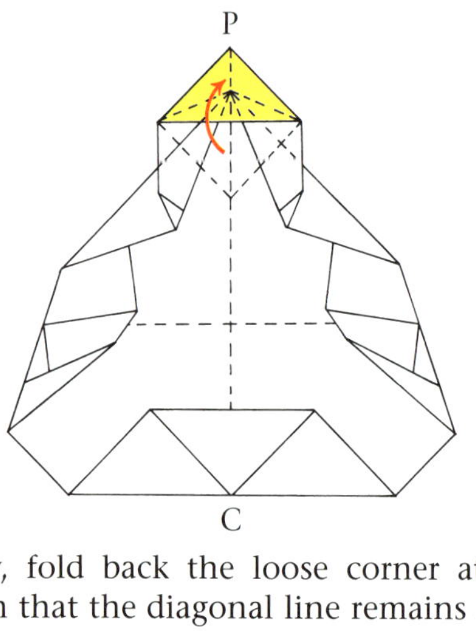

9.

9. Lastly, fold back the loose corner at (P). Pay attention that the diagonal line remains straight.

Assemble according to instructions for a 5-rayed form (see page 16). If you do not glue the tips, the loose folds will appear slightly three-dimensional. Some of the inner contours then remain indistinct and give a dreamy nuance. If you glue down the points, then the subtle triangles become more prominent as if each point is wearing a cover or Chinese hat.

9. Star Blossoms *

figure with 5 rays
diameter:
31 cm (12.2") Cut 1
21 cm (8.25") Cut 5
15 cm (5.9") Cut 2

Featherlight, like apple blossoms in a spring breeze, these little stars are similarly light and simple to construct.

Fold diagonals very carefully in 5 squares.

For the light stars, white tissue paper was given a light wash of pink or blue with a damp sponge. The inner stars at the center were intensified with color after the stars were assembled. >

1.

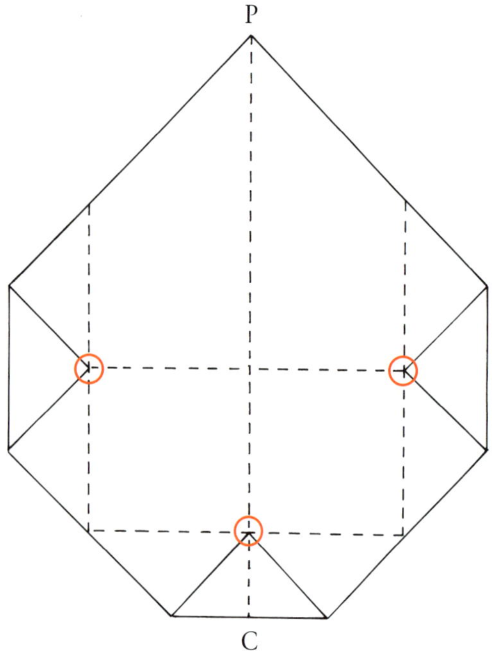

1. Look at the step 1 and step 2 diagrams for Light and Airy (page 30). For this pattern, fold the (C) and side wing points according to that pattern. Glue these three points.

The blue tissue paper for this star was sprinkled with fine water drops.

2.

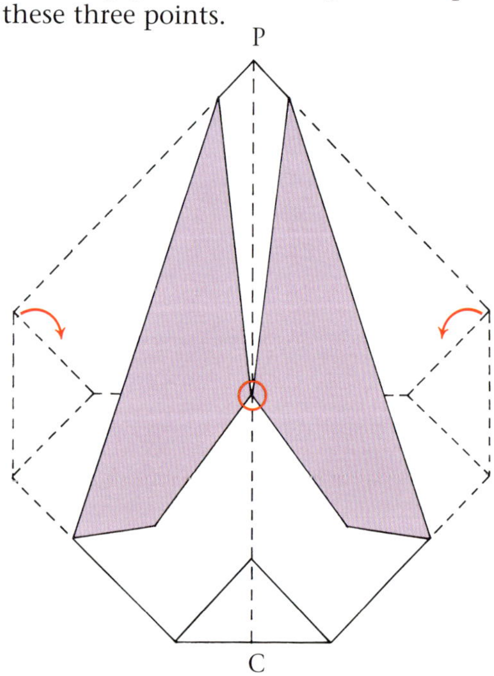

2. Fold side wings again toward the midpoint and glue them at the point.

Assemble according to instructions for a 5-rayed pattern (see page 16). Be sure that the midlines at (C) on each of the 5 segments meet exactly at the center.

10. Sun Medallion ****

figure with 11 rays
diameter:
37 cm (14.6") Cut 4
29 cm (11.4") Cut 1

Some color was removed from the bright red (carmine) tissue paper with a damp sponge to give the warm rays greater contrast.

From this unusual number of 11 rays, an especially harmonious sun splendor can be created. Long rays alternate with short strong "star pillars." This dynamic alternation is held in calm balance by the delicate central rosette.

Take 11 pieces of paper in the dimensions indicated above.

Folding for this transparency is a direct continuation of the previous star pattern.

First fold the diagonal lines and the support lines (see Light and Airy steps 1 and 2, p.30). Then fold as for Star Blossom through steps 1 and 2 (p. 42); but *do not glue the (c) point and do not glue the side wings to the midpoint yet*. Having come this far with your eleven segments, simply rotate the piece so that *the* (P) *point becomes the* (C) *point and vice versa.*

1. Fold the (C) point to the midpoint to create a support line, then open it back out. Fold down the upper edge of the side wings as shown in the diagram. Now glue the side wings at the midpoint.

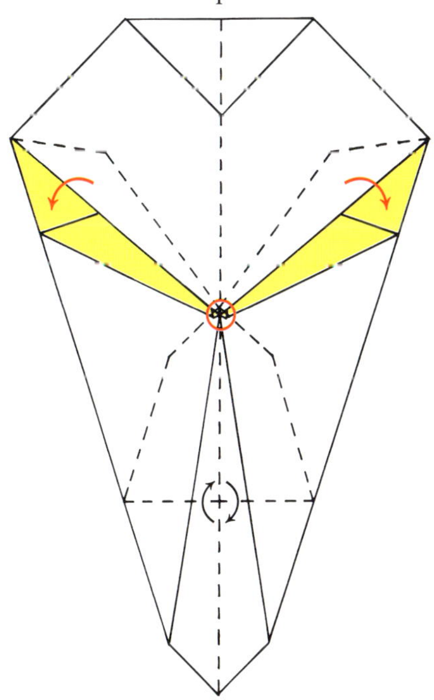

1.

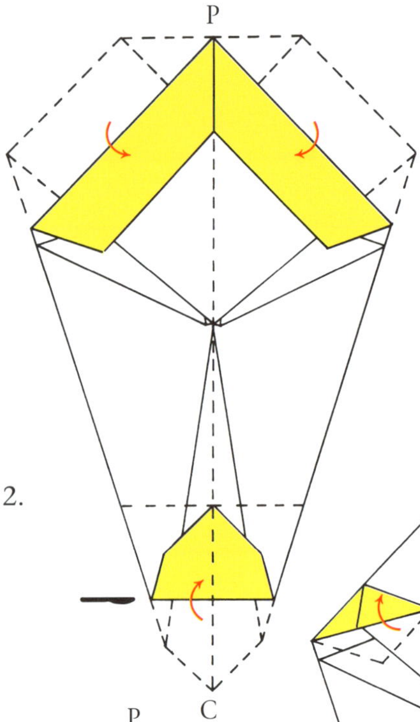

2.

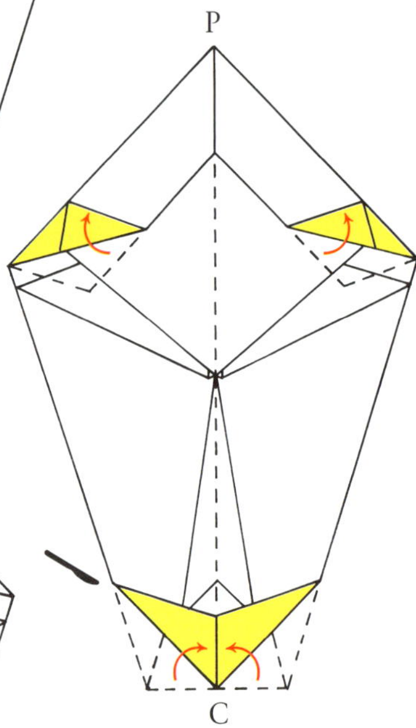

3.

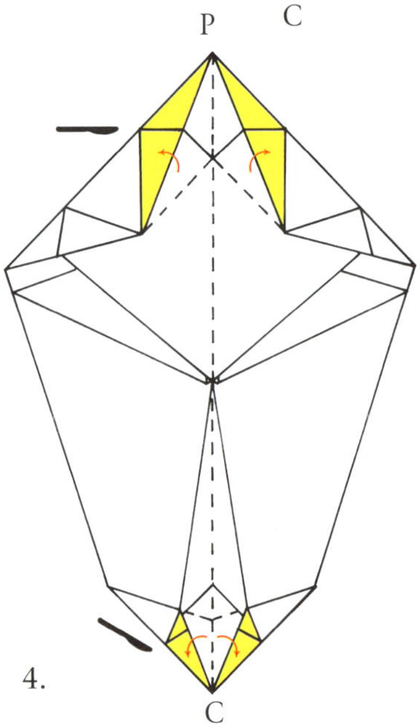

4.

2–4. Fold according to the diagrams, creasing with the back of the knife as needed.

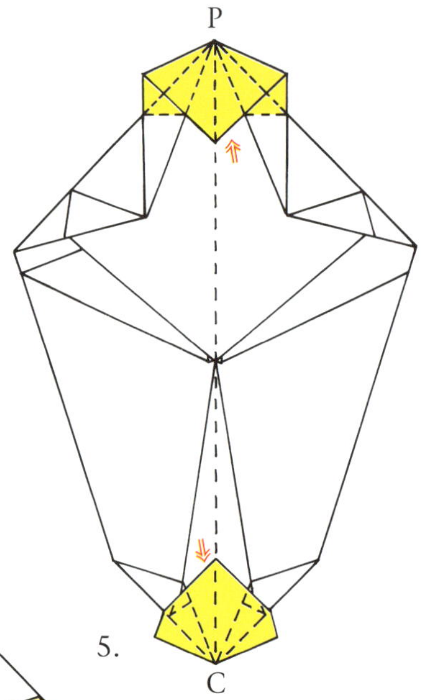

5.

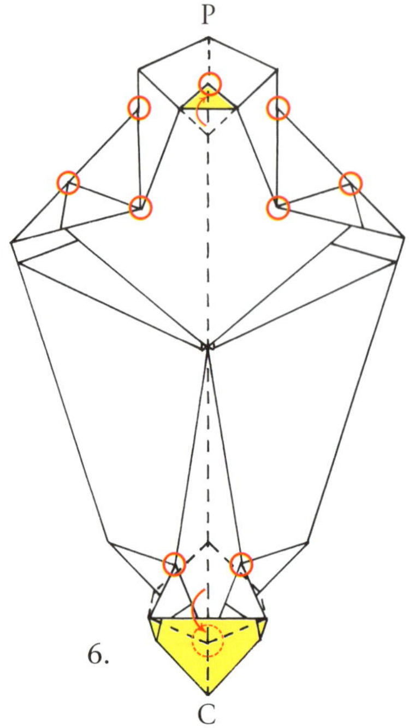

6.

5. Pull gently on the loose (C) corner, freeing the folds. Be sure that the point is on the midline when you crease this fold. Follow the same procedure for (P).

6. Fold the loose (C) point back as far as possible. Very exact folding is necessary for successful assembly. The midline must run very straight from the tip to the center. Make the last fold at (P). Apply a dot of glue at all the indicated places.

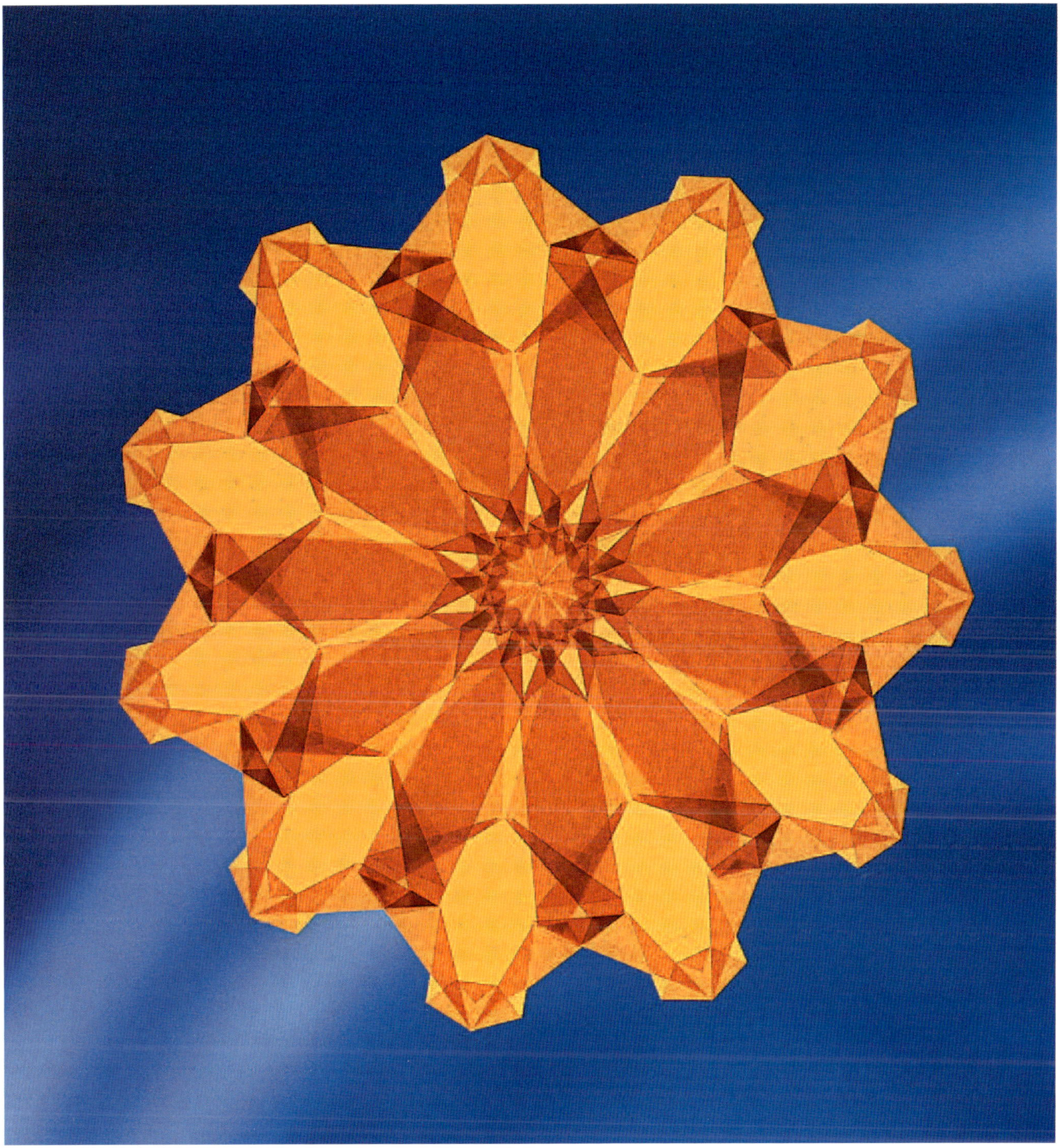

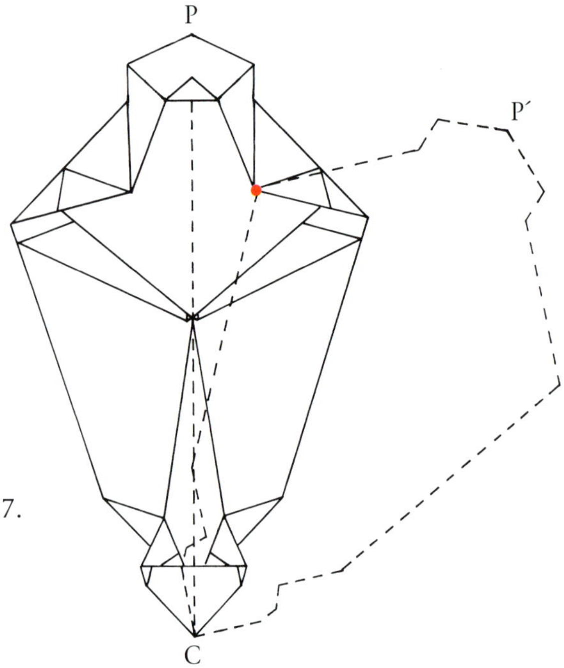

7.

11. Ice Flower ****

figure with 6 rays
diameter:
37 cm (14.6") Cut 4
29 cm (11.4") Cut 1

The folding technique for this Ice Flower is similar to that for Sun Medallion. However, its clear coolness puts us in a quiet winter mood.

1–3. Fold diagonals in 6 squares. Fold as indicated in the diagrams.

1.

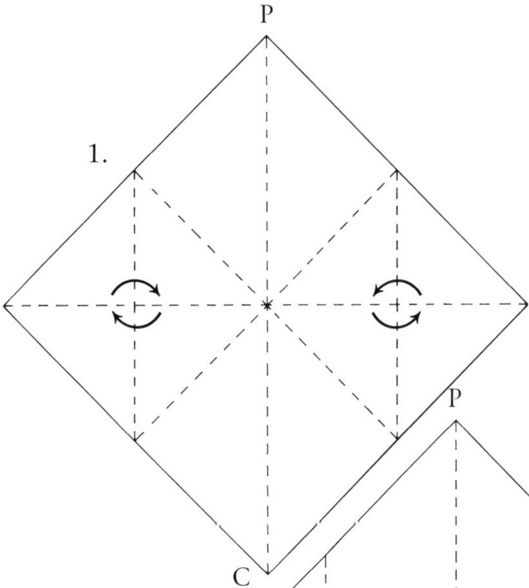

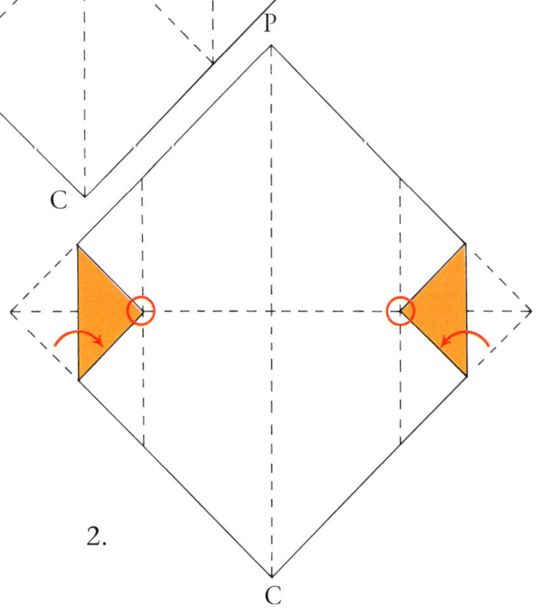

2.

7. Now comes the unusual assembly of the eleven rays (see instructions, p. 16). The diagram indicates the assembly of 2 segments. The important orientation point for cut 4 is approximately 1/8″ (2 mm) from the edge of the right fold at (P). For cut 1, the point is only about 1/16″ (1 mm) from that edge.

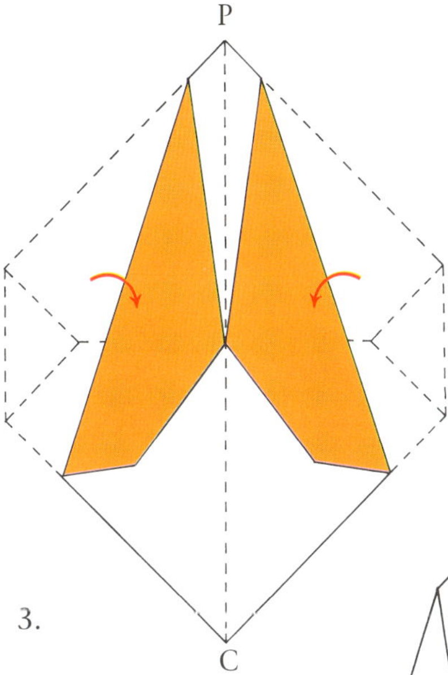

3.

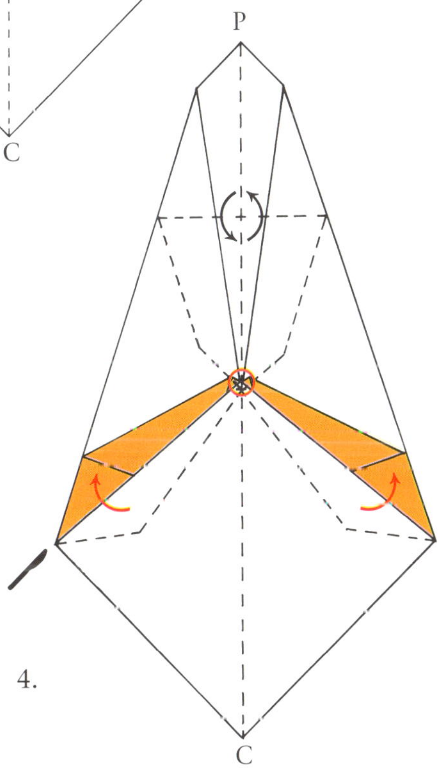

4.

4. Fold (P) to the midpoint and open again to form a support line. Fold back the lower corners of the wings. Glue wings at the midpoint.

Some color was removed from the dark cobalt blue tissue paper with a damp sponge.

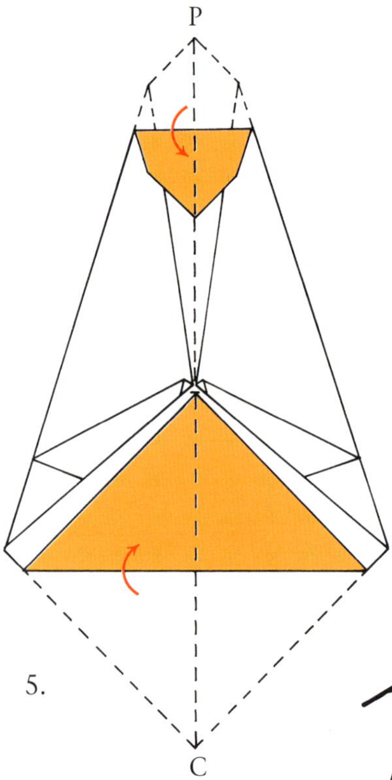

5.

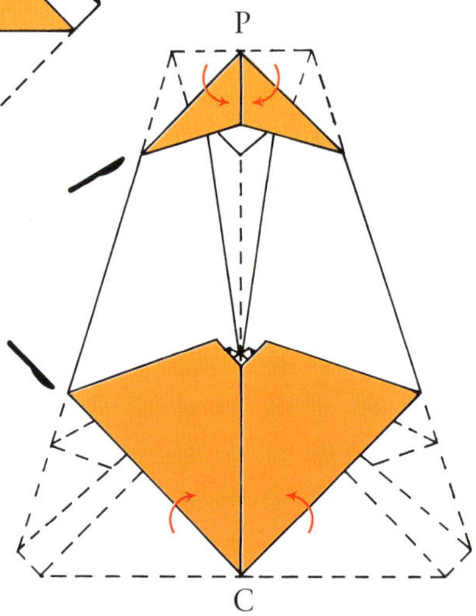

6.

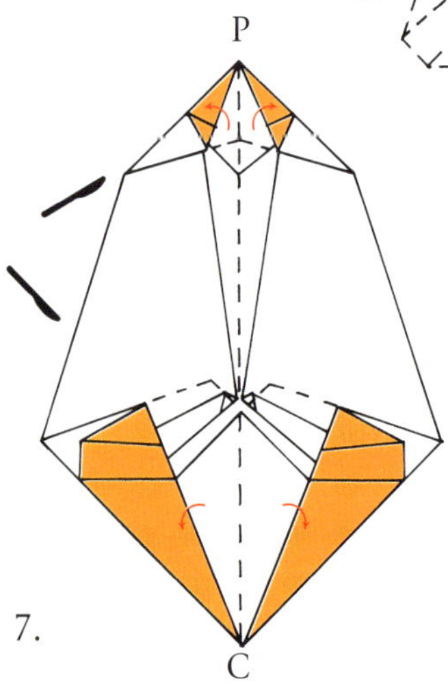

7.

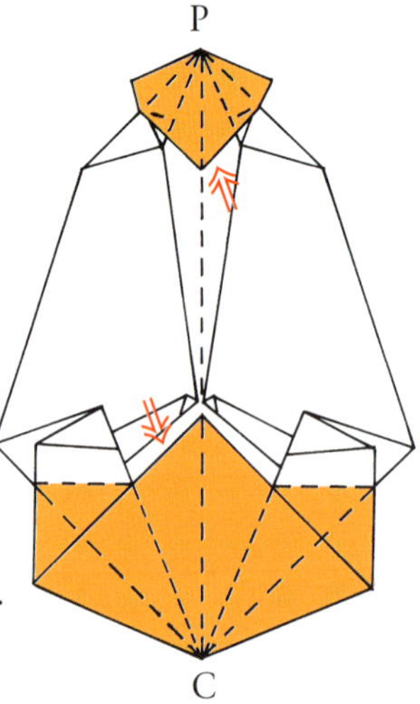

8.

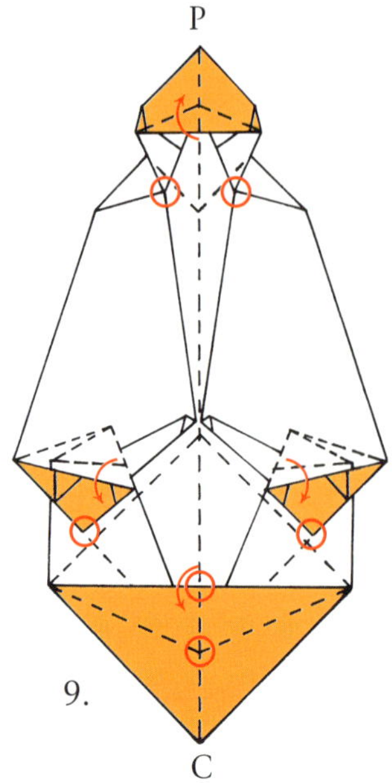

9.

5–7. Continue folding according to the diagrams, creasing with the knife as needed.

8. Gently pull at the center point (C) and reveal the concealed folds, making sure to allign the midlines before creasing the new folds. Proceed in the same way for point (P).

9. Fold out points at (C) and (P), still keeping the midlines very straight. Fold down the last corners of the side sections away from the middle. Glue at the indicated places.

Assemble according to instructions for a 6-rayed figure (see page 16).

To achieve the wonderful mauve shade for this crystal, a sheet of light pink tissue paper was used. Starting in the mid-section, dark lilac watercolor was applied in decreasing concentration toward the center. >

12. *Warmth in Motion* ***

figure with 9 rays
diameter:
37 cm (14.6") Cut 4
27.5 cm (10.8") Cut 1
18.5 cm (7.3") Cut 5

These flickering flames of tissue paper move like an ever-travelling sphere of warmth through a summer breeze. The free, airy folds of these nine segment forms lift their circling movements to three-dimensional completion.

Make only one diagonal fold in each of 9 squares and proceed with step-by-step instructions.

1–4. Fold according to the diagrams, using the back of a knife to crease the edges.

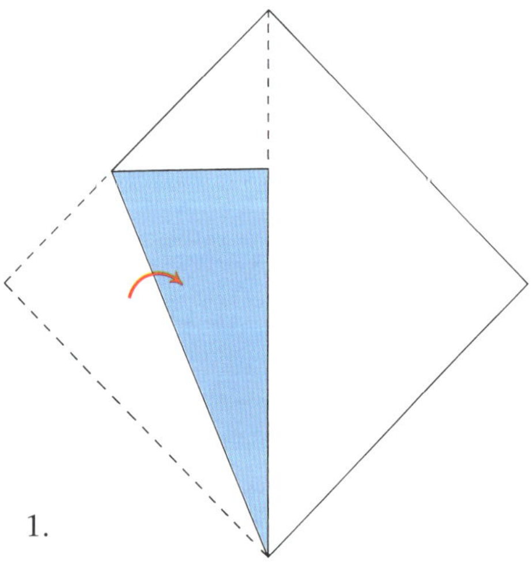

1.

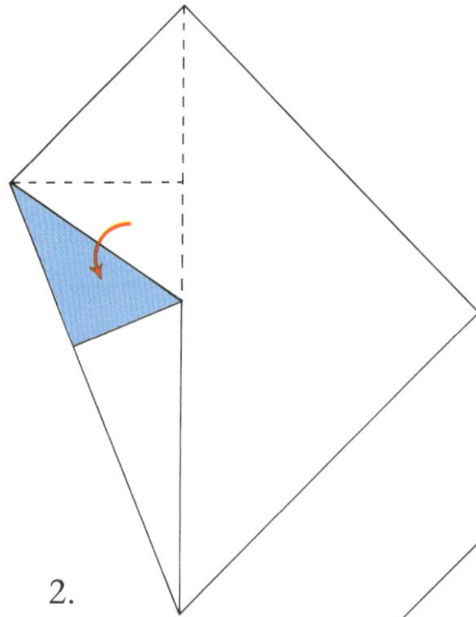

2.

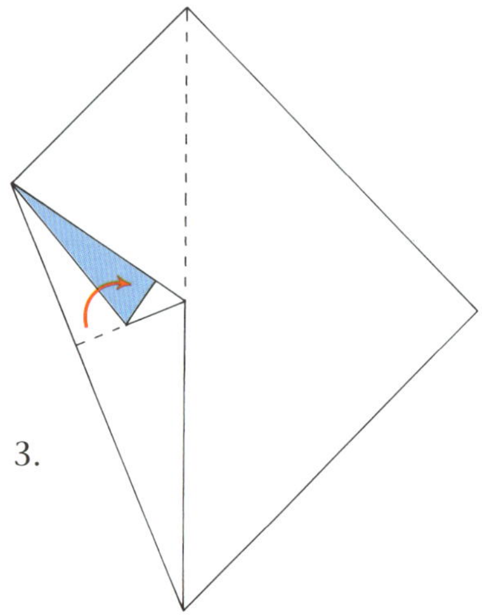

3.

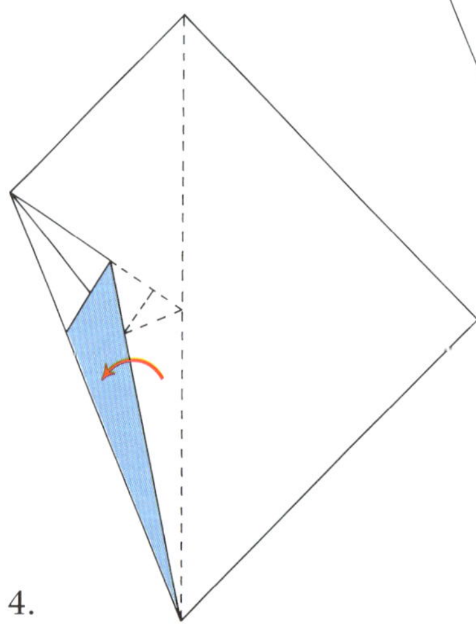

4.

The orange tones of the smaller transparency were obtained by light applications of dark orange water-color. >

In order to give the impression of movement, not only in form but also in color, the segments are made in several yellow tones and white.

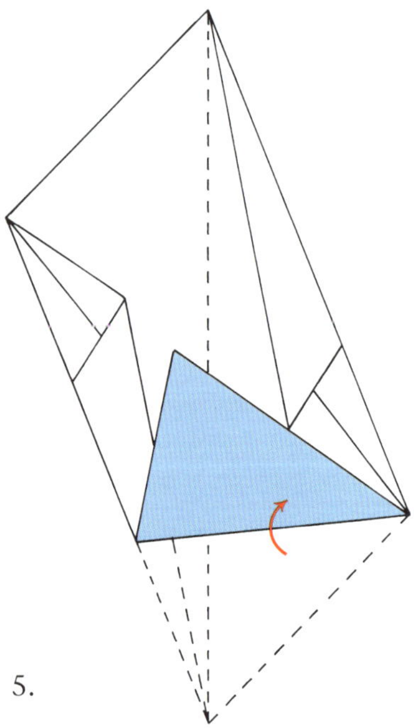

5.

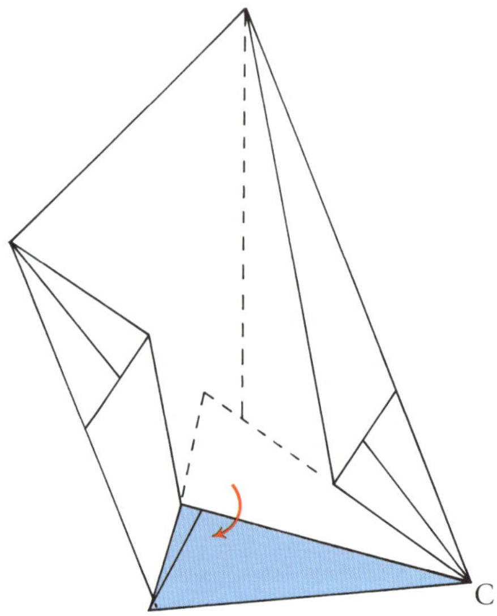

6.

5. *Fold the second half of the segment as you did in steps 1-4 but reversed as in a mirror.* Fold the lower right edge up to meet the right inward-folded point as shown.

6. Make the final fold according to the diagram. *The point at the right becomes the* (C) *point.* To emphasize the three-dimensional quality, no glue is used.

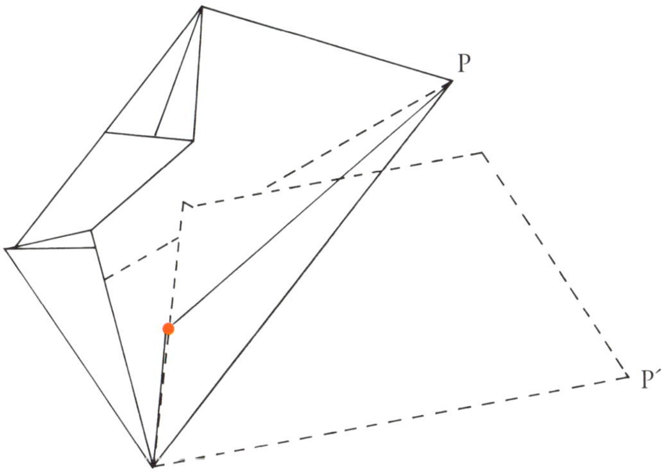

7.

7. Assemble the 9 segments, with the left edge of the second segment glued very close to the right inner edge of the first. However, you must leave a tiny space between these edges (1/8″ for cut 4, 1/16″ for cuts 1 and 5). *Be very careful not to glue down the loose fold at the center.*

The diagram indicates the assembly of 2 segments.

In this transparency, different orange shades and two yellow segments were used. To enliven the effect, some of the color was removed from the paper with a damp sponge before folding. Some of the yellow segments were tinted by stacking different colored pieces on top of each other and dabbing them with a damp sponge.

13. *Flying Rays* **

figure with 5 rays
diameter:
24.5 cm (9.6") Cut 1
18 cm (7") Cut 5

Delicate star-tips glitter like gems that appear at the window rising toward the sky! Leaving the folds unglued gives a decorative three-dimensional effect.

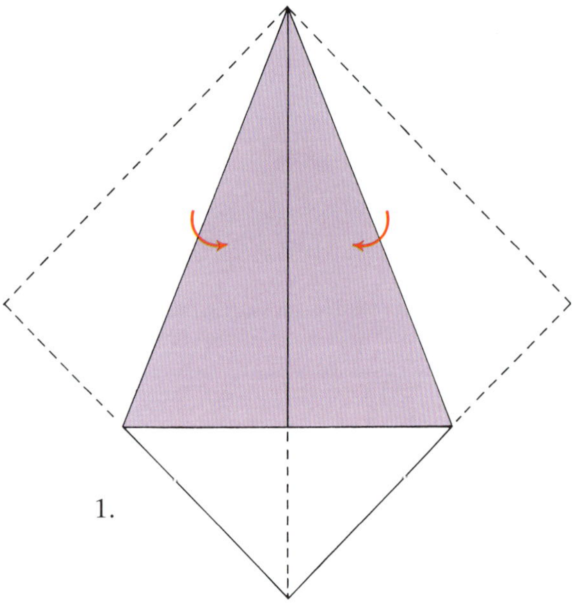

1.

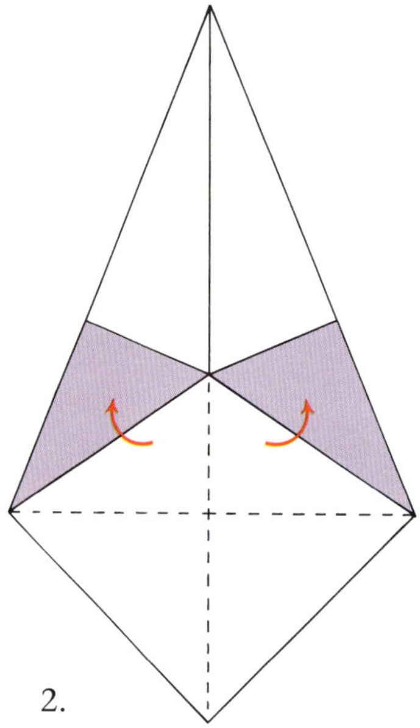

2.

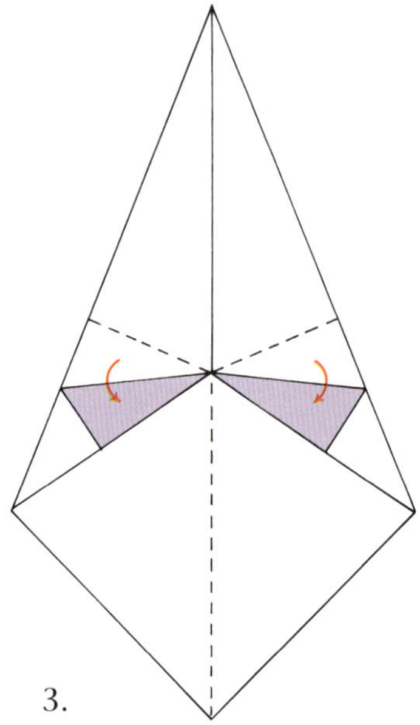

3.

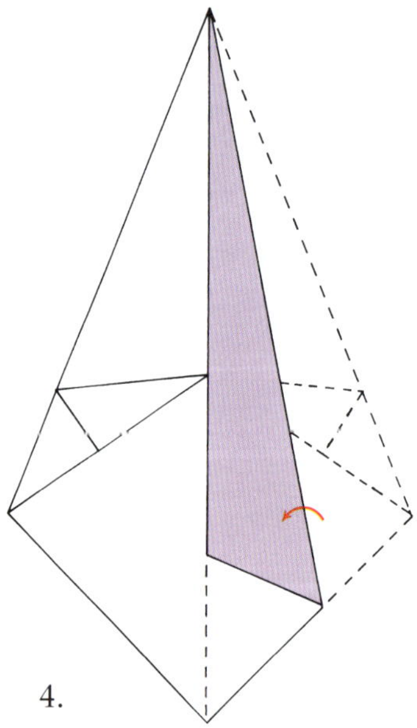

4.

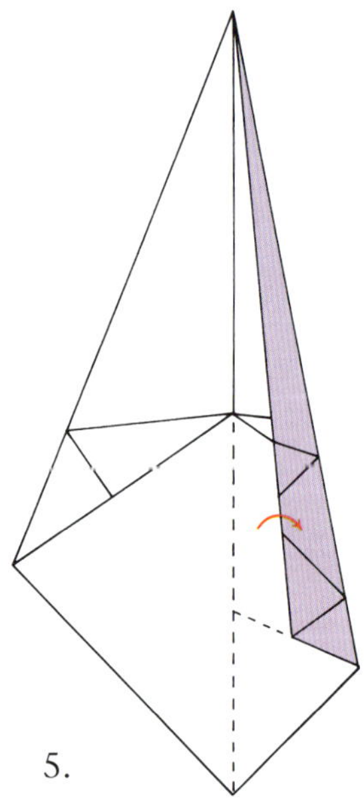

5.

1–7. Fold one diagonal in each of 5 squares. Continue folding according to the diagrams. It is helpful to crease the folds with the back of a knife to create perfect sharp points at the tips. Achieving these sharp points requires a good deal of dexterity when making the small version of this pattern.

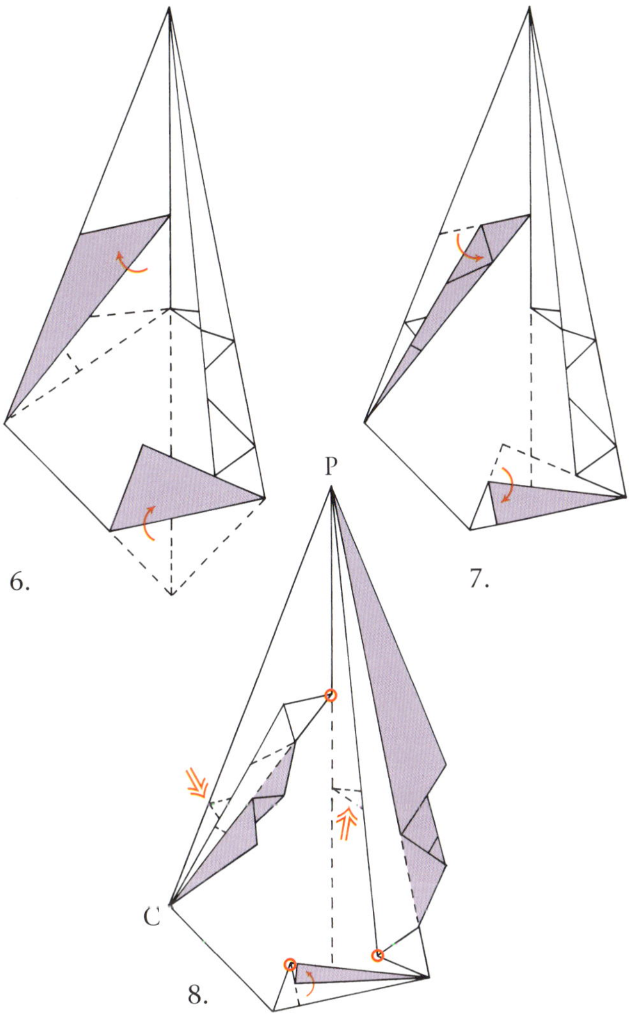

8. Make the fold at the bottom. Gently pull out the middle corner, in order to fold the right side of the segment to the outside. Open the left side in the same way but down to the inside. Glue the three indicated places.

The left angle becomes the (C) *center*. Assemble the 5 segments with the help of the diagram. An exception here is that the left edge serves as the midline. (See basic instructions, page 16.)

The small star was created with clear sky blue tissue paper. The folds of the other star were glued. A little of the yellow color was extracted from the paper and a touch of orange watercolor added.

14. Star in the Sun ***

figure with 5 rays
diameter:
36 cm (14.2") Cut 4 and Cut 1
26 cm (10.2") Cut 1 and Cut 5

In the midst of a swirl of rays in two colors, a five-pointed star appears with partly dissolved edges. This calm center makes a sharp contrast with the swirl of surrounding points.

This dynamic transparency is created from two different-sized sets of Flying Rays (p. 54). Using two harmonizing colors can make a rich contrast in the rays. Experiment with cooler colors like pink, blue, and lilac or warm colors like yellow, orange, and red.

Lavender blue and pink tissue paper combine for a calm radiating effect.

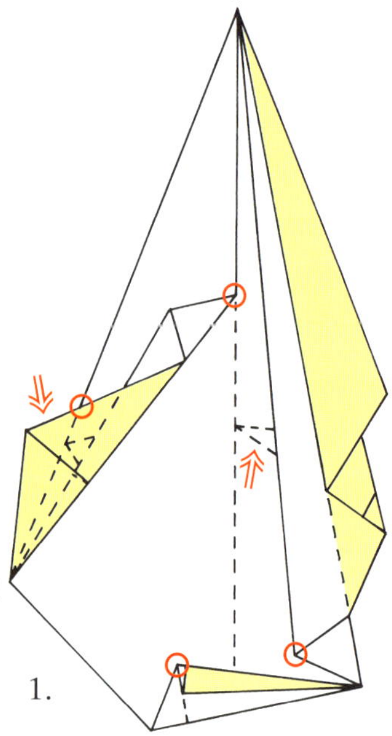

Fold 5 large and 5 small segments according to instructions 1–7 for Flying Rays (p. 54). *Only then do you unfold the 5 larger segments according to step 8.*

1. For the 5 small rays, follow step 8 except for the left side, which is folded outward and glued. The right and bottom folds remain unchanged. Glue all four points.

2. Before assembling the whole star, use glue streaks to join each large segment to a small segment as a pair according to the diagram. The right corner of the large segment lies on top of the unfolded right side of the small one. Glue at the point marked with a circle (⦿). The drawing shows precisely how to assemble each pair.

Now assemble the 5 folded pairs as indicated for Flying Rays (see instructions, p. 16).

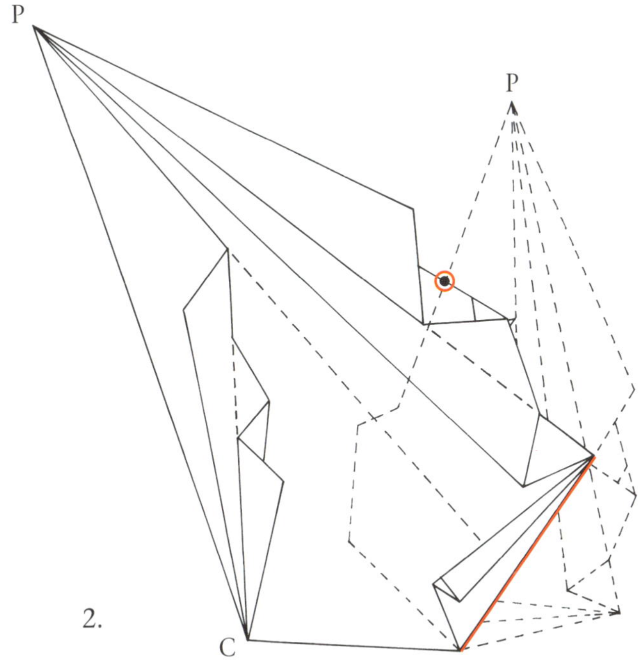

2.

Make this fiery bundle of rays by extracting some color from two stacked layers of yellow and dark orange tissue paper.

15. Forest Glen ***

40 cm (15.7") long, Cut 4 and Cut 1

A forest glen dressed in green and blue tones. We use the same folding pattern as with the previous two transparencies, but assembled differently. These trees bring the refreshing call of the forest right into the house.

Take 3 squares of cut 4, and 4 squares of cut 1. Fold each following the instructions for Flying Rays up through step 8 (see page 54). *Do not unfold the right sides of the smaller pieces as they will serve as supporting elements for the assembly.*

First glue together 3 pairs of large and small trees (small on left, large on right). The tip of the small tree is guided under the loose fold of the large tree from below upwards and then glued to the outer edge (marked in red). Then glue two pairs together (from left: small–large, small–large), followed by a small tree glued to the right side of the large tree on the right of the group already joined. Finally add the last pair of trees. The diagram shows the glue points.

Consolidate the total structure with glue on the back side. Three-dimensional effects can be created by gluing folds shut or opening them up. Interesting perspectives can arise through the color play as well as through the relationships of the trees to one another.

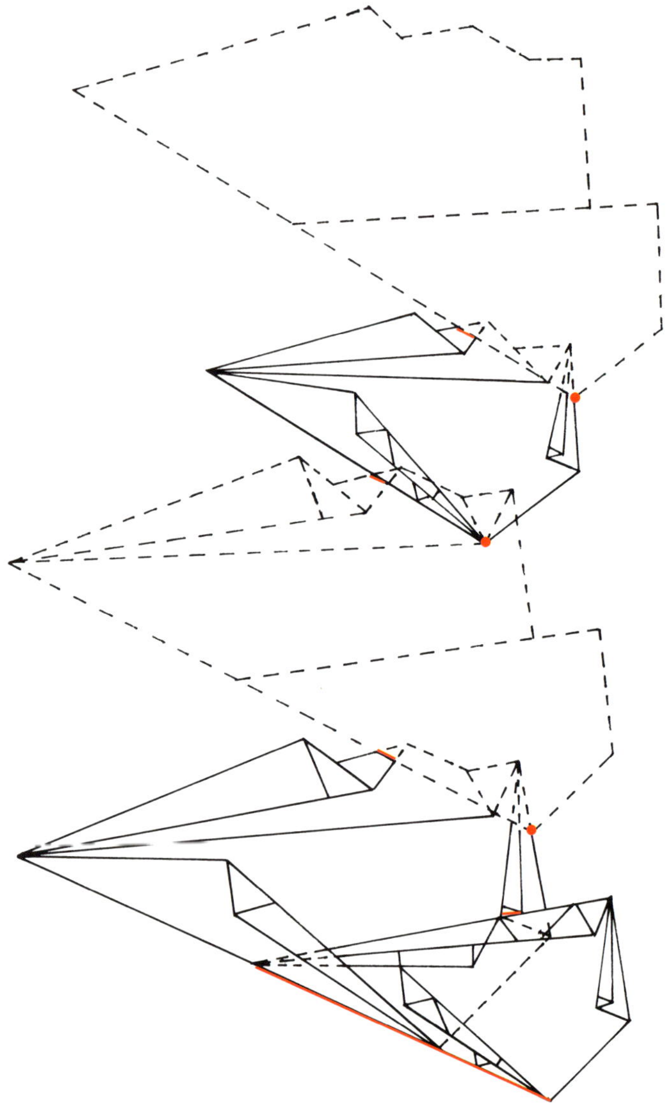

Blue and green tones suggest the play of sunlight on > calm forest trees.

16. Tourmaline ****

figure with 6 rays
diameter:
33 cm (13") Cut 4
24 cm (9.4") Cut 1

Through the play of the triangles, this amazing transparency reminds us of a tourmaline cross-section. In its heart, the six-pointed star of light and shadow makes a precious star within the precious stone.

1–3. Fold both diagonals in each of 6 squares. Fold one side of the segment according to the diagrams. *Then form the second side in the same manner.* Crease each fold with the back of a knife to avoid any slippage of the lower fold.

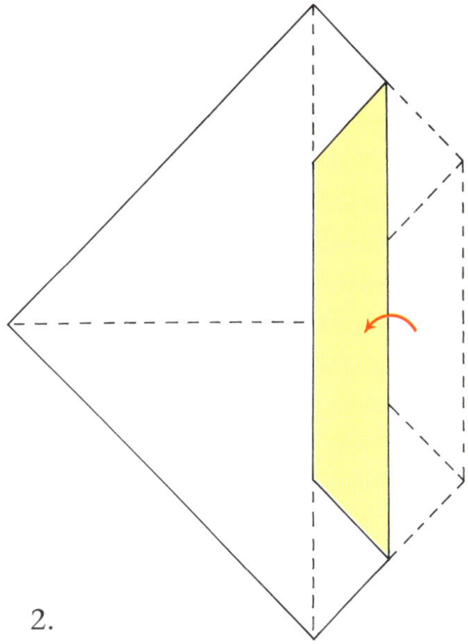

2.

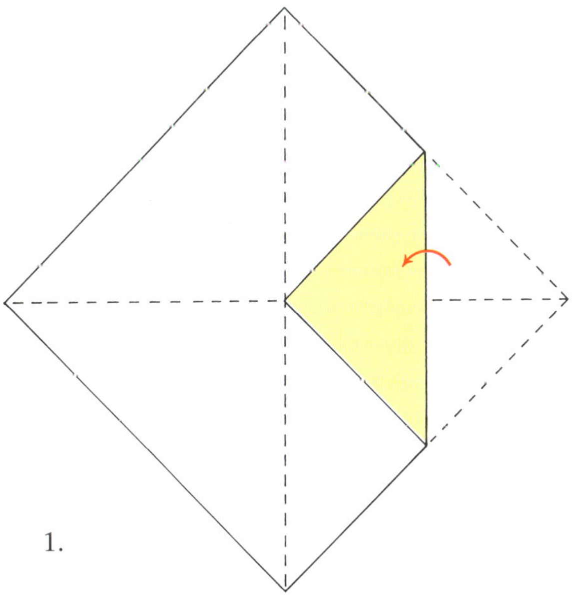

1.

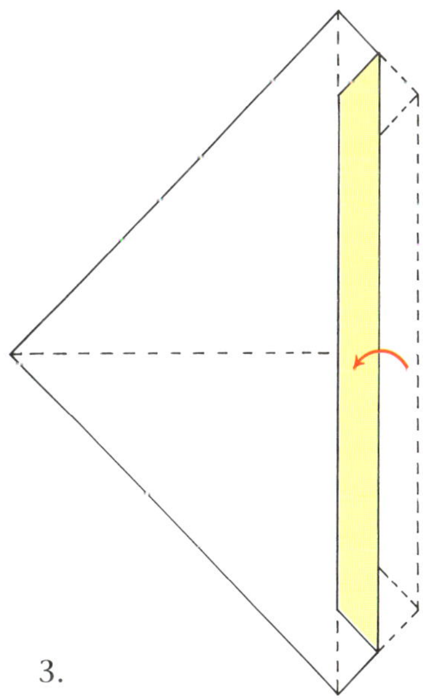

3.

This pink transparency was sprinkled with water drops.

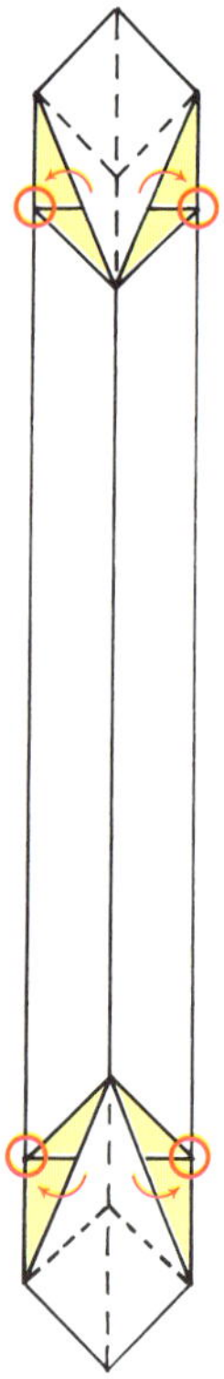

4.

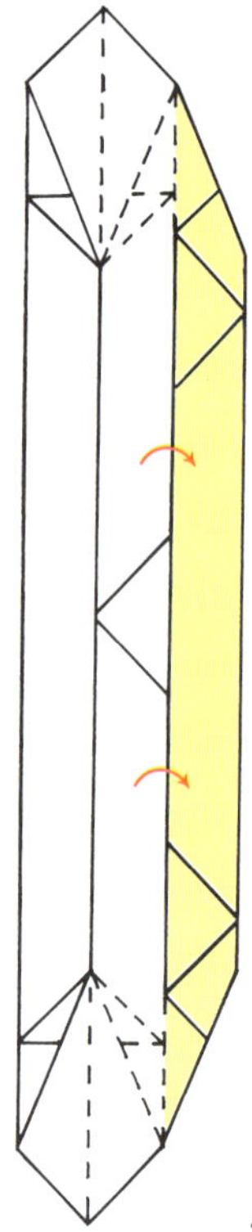

5.

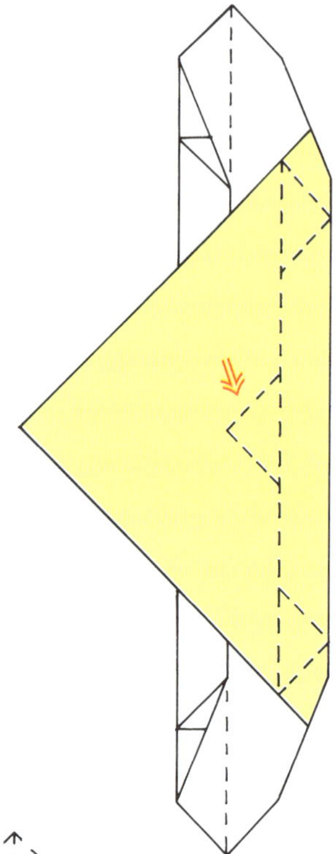

6.

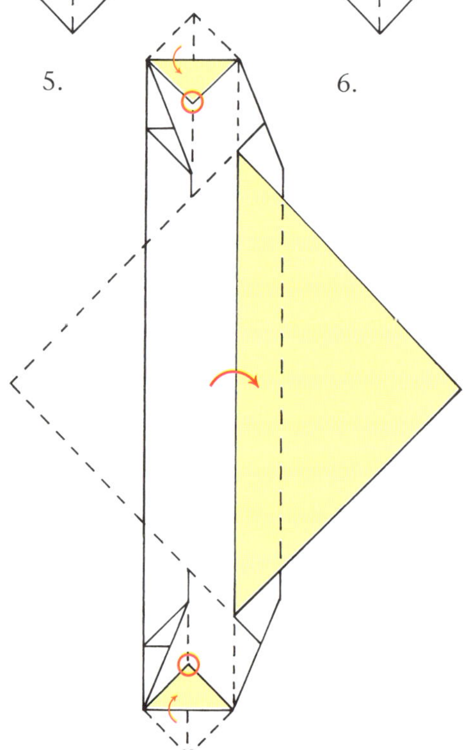

7.

4. Fold down the four corners and glue them.

5. Again, proceed folding one side at a time. Unfold the right side, exposing the triangle at the center.

6. Pull this triangle out and lay it flat to the left.

7. Fold this section back again to the right. Fold the top and bottom points down carefully to the midline and glue them.

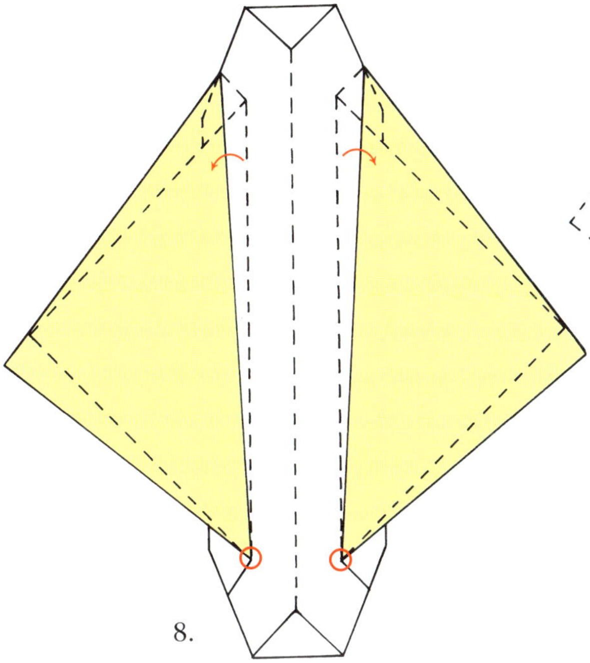
8.

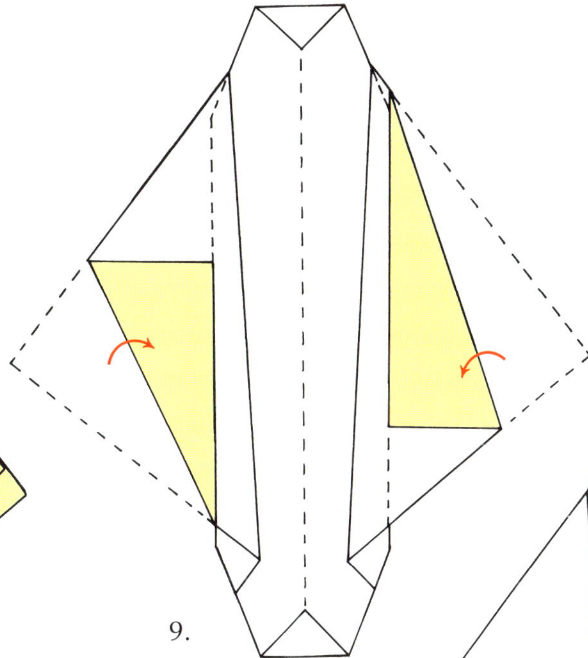
9.

8. *Repeat this process on the other half of the segment.* Reposition the side folds slanting them outward a little at the top. Glue side wings at the bottom glue points.

9. Fold side wings (one up from the bottom, the other down from the top) to the line *above the edges of the fold underneath.*

10–11. Fold according to diagrams and then glue at 4 places. *The right wing point becomes the* (C) *center.*

Assemble the 6 segments using the template on page 16. *The upper left corner becomes the point (P) and is placed on the diagonal line of the template.*

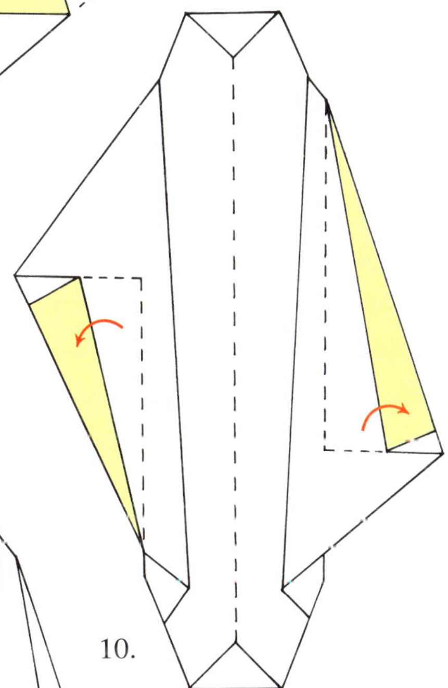
10.

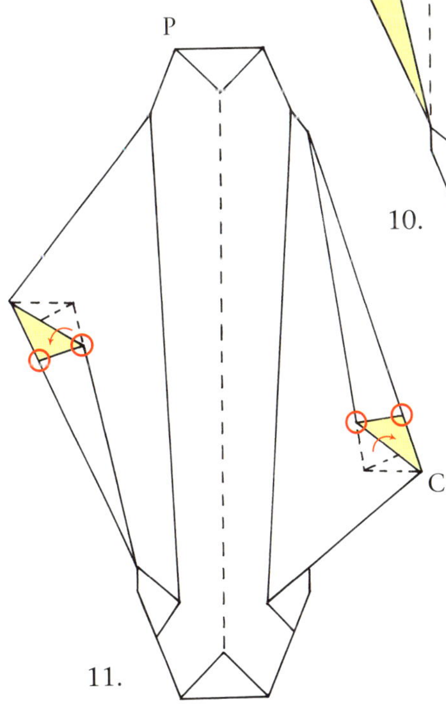

11.

17. Five-star Fun *

figure with 5 rays
diameter:
31 cm (12.2") Cut 1
21 cm (8.25") Cut 5
15 cm (5.9") Cut 2

The structure of this classic five-star is clear; its static quality, however, is only relative. By observing it carefully, we can feel drawn into a slow, deepening rotary motion created by the interplay of alternating light and dark star forms.

Fold two diagonals carefully in 5 squares. For the (C) center, fold as for Light and Airy diagrams 1 and 2 (see page 30).

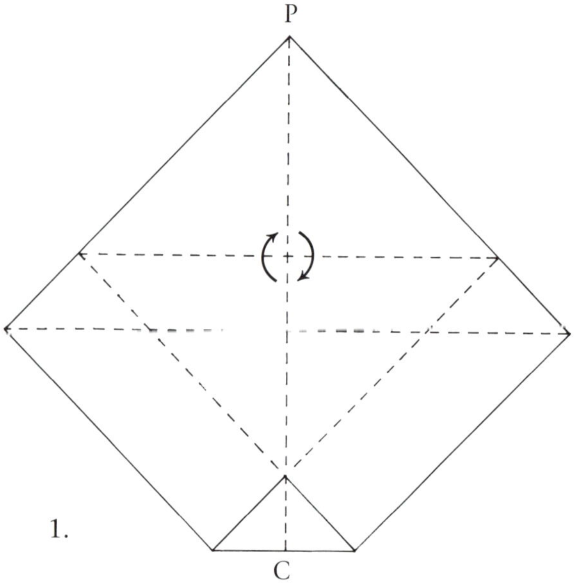

1.

1. Fold the top point down to the upturned bottom point and open again, making a support fold.

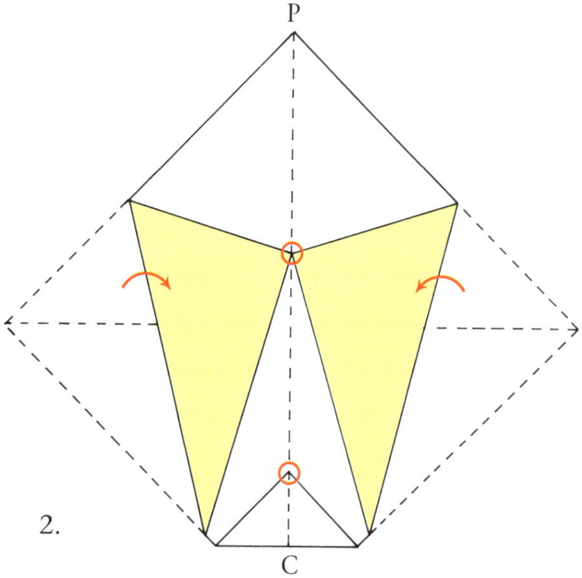

2.

2. Fold both side wings to the midline. Glue side and bottom points.

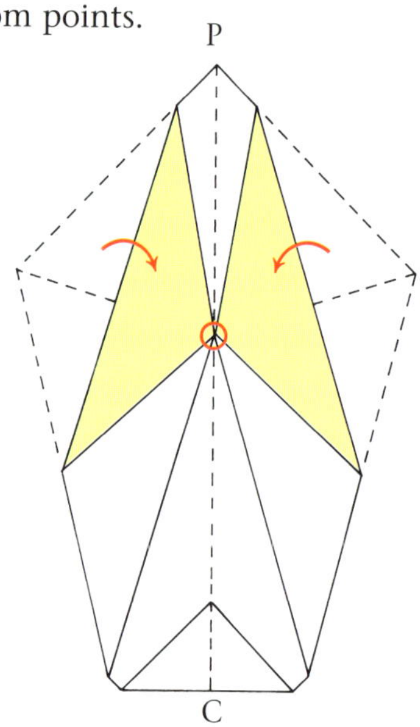

3.

3. Make final folds in the side wings and crease with the back of a knife.

Assemble following the directions for a 5-pointed figure (page 16). Be careful to join the midlines (C) exactly at the center.

For this star, lavender tissue paper was evenly colored with a touch of light blue, using a small sponge. >

This fan in white tissue paper conjures up a play of colors when viewed through a window. Watercolor paint was applied to appropriate angles before the folding process.

18. Shimmering Fan ***

figure with 9 rays
41.5 cm (16.3") Cut 4
30 cm (11.8") Cut 1

This fan transparency with its open folds spread in an arc seems to bring a fresh breeze on a hot summer day.

Of the 9 segments, the outer two will have additional folds.

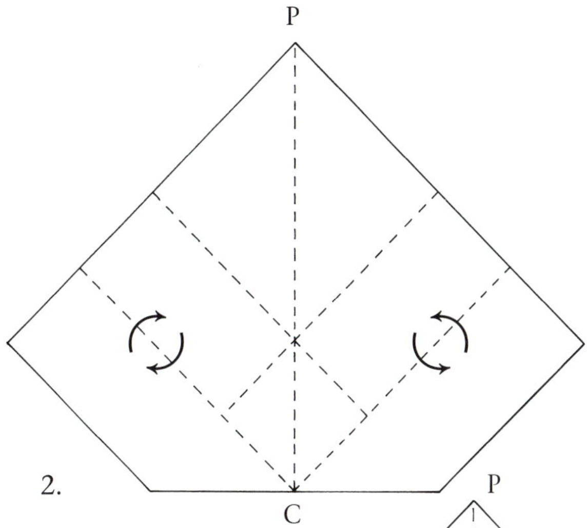

2.

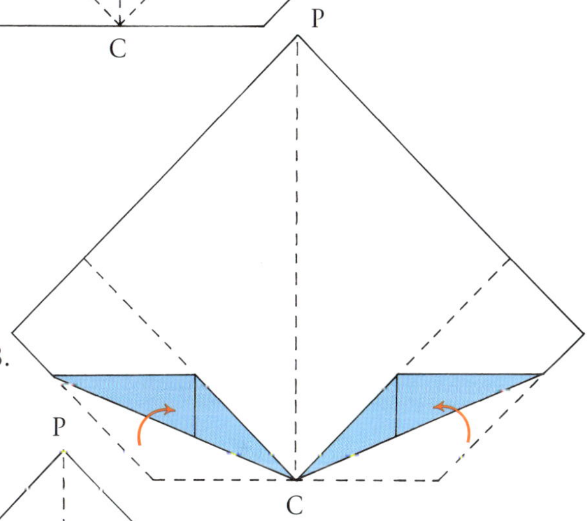

3.

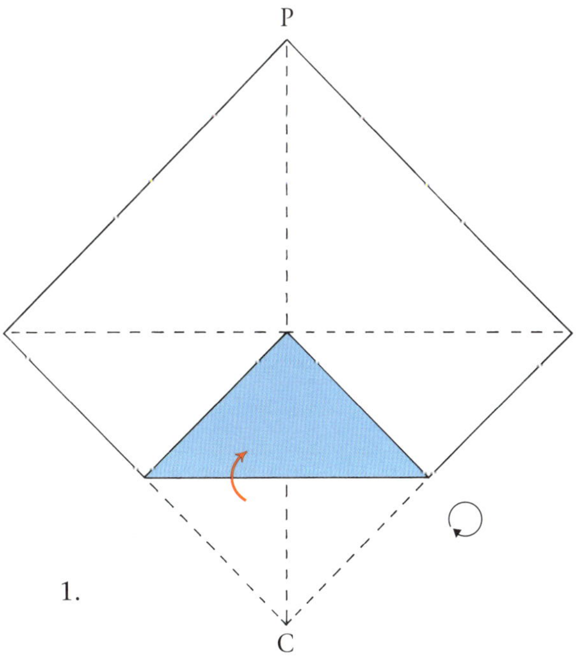

1.

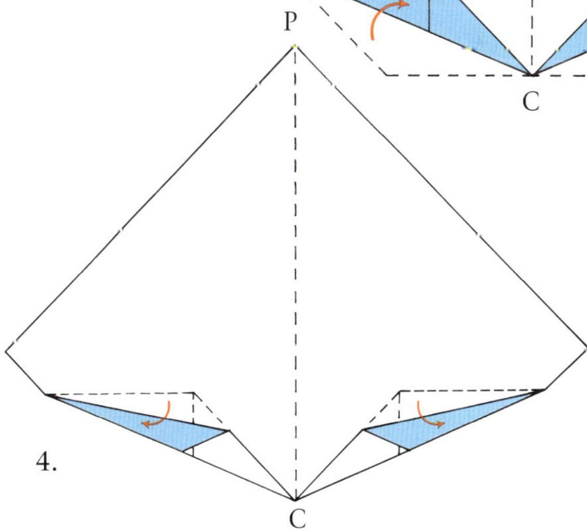

4.

1. Make 2 diagonal folds in each of 9 squares. Fold the (C) point to the center *and then turn the piece over.*

2–4. Continue folding this reverse side according to the diagrams.

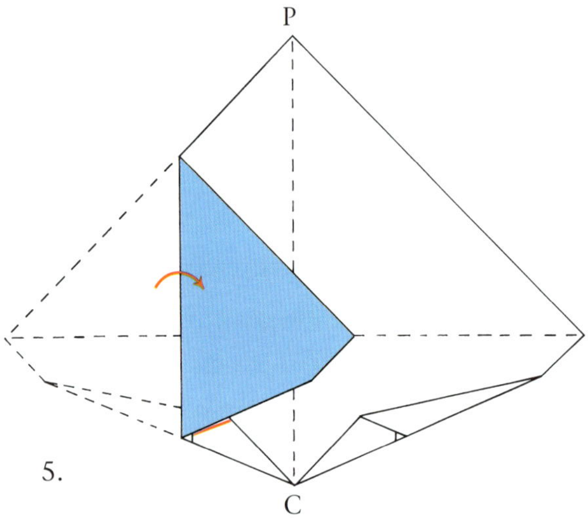

5.

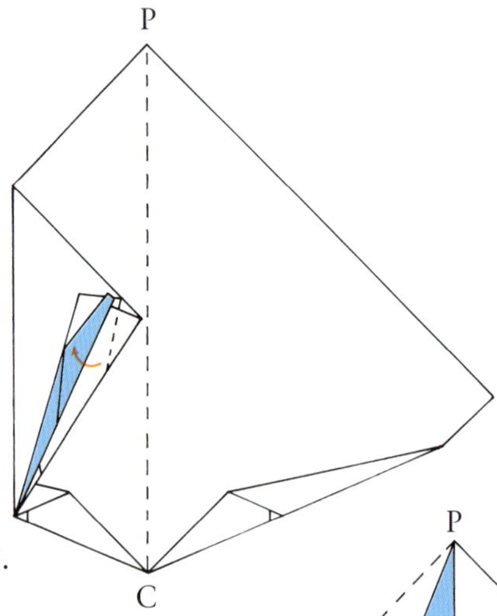

8.

5. Fold the left wing, guided by the lower fold to the left of the (C) point, marked with a red line.

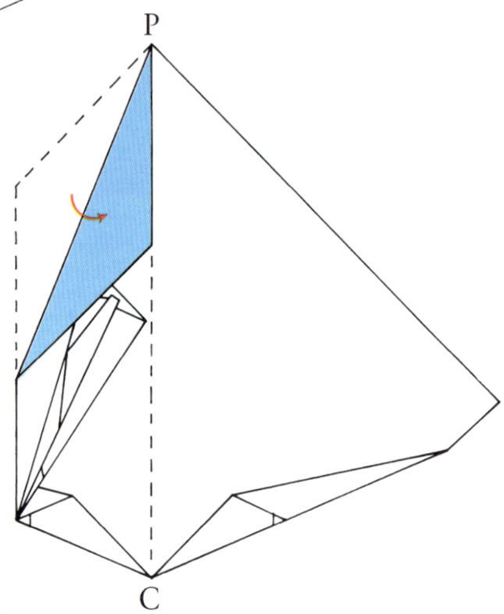

9.

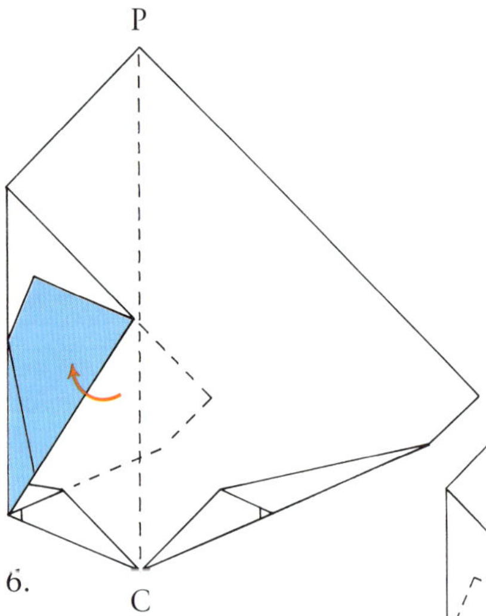

6.

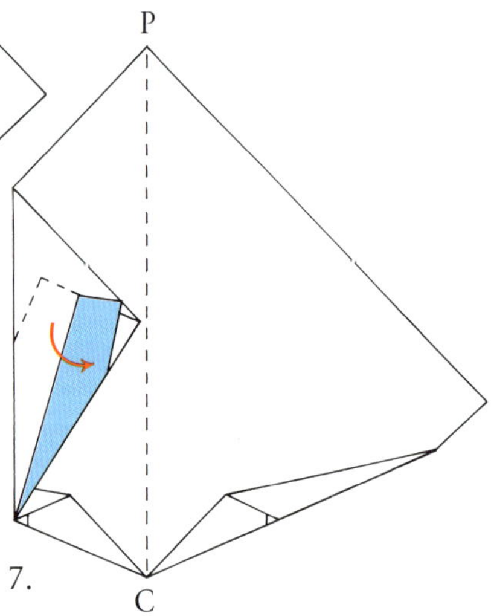

7.

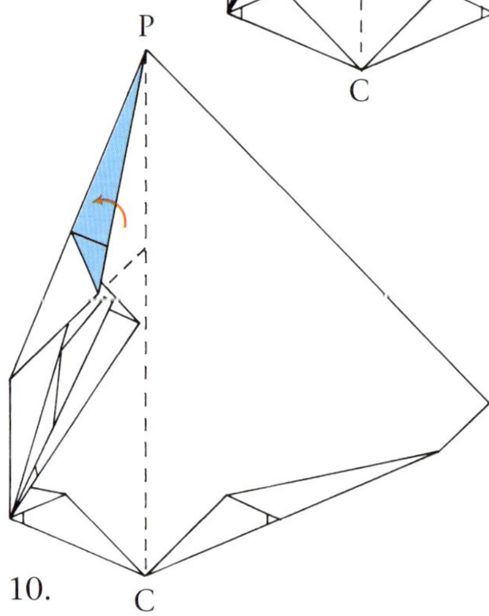

10.

6–8. Continue folding according to the diagrams. *Repeat the same process for the right side, beginning from step 5.*

For the outer right and left segments of the fan:
9–10. Do additional folds for the left side of the fan according to the diagrams.

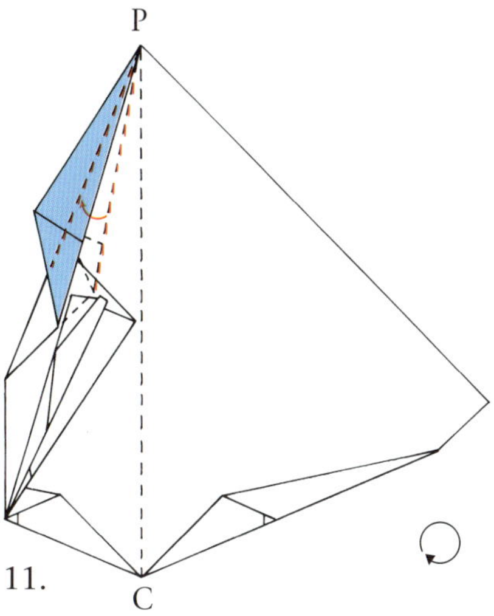

11.

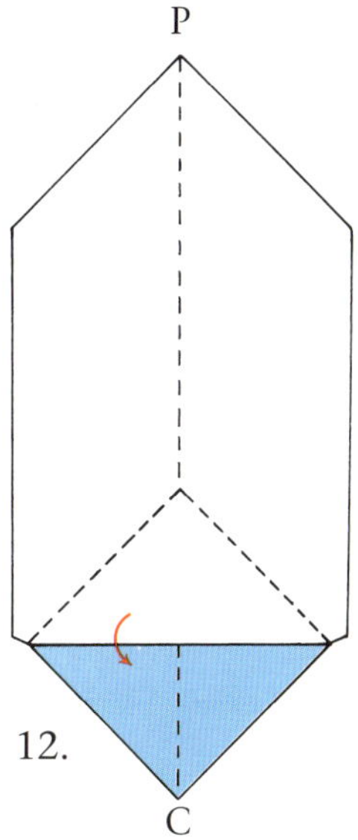

12.

11. Diagram 11 shows that in order to get a firm end fold, the inner edge must be moved outwards and laid flat on the outer edge below. *For the right side of the fan, fold another segment in a mirror image of the left one.*

12. *Turn all segments over for the last fold.*

13. Assemble the transparency beginning with the center segment and adding to the right and left sides. The centers are glued together so that the glue point of the second segment is on (C) to connect it from below to the (C) of the previous segment. The orientation point is on the right and left lower edge of the segment (see dot (⦿) in the diagram).

Add the right and left segments last.

Secure the structure with a few glue lines on the back. The front is not glued so the folds can be pulled out a little to heighten the three-dimensional effect.

This sea blue transparency is made of 5 light blue segments in the middle and 4 darker ones on the sides. The marbelled effect was created by stacking three different blue papers that had first been sprinkled with water drops.

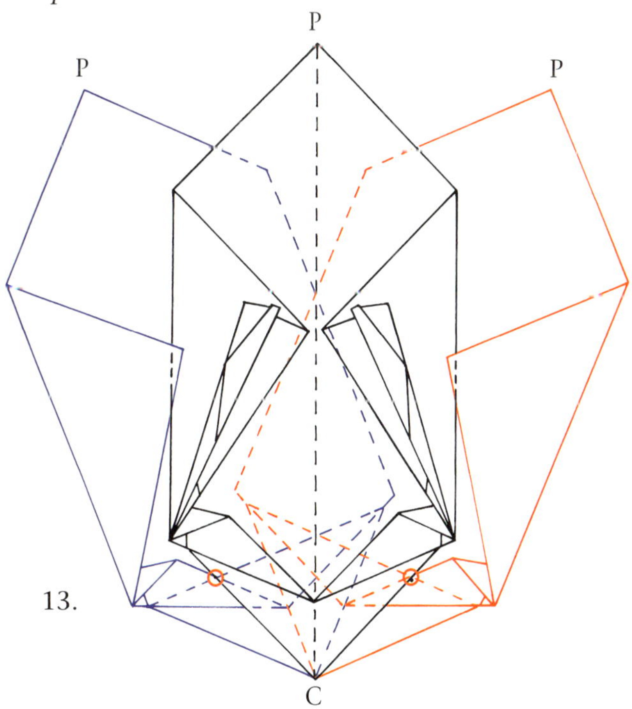

13.

19. Crisscross *****

figure with 4 rays
diameter:
41 cm (16.1") Cut 3
29 cm (11.4") Cut 4

This transparency with its folded back points, transverse lines and cross motifs is reminiscent of the ground plan of cloister gardens.

This cross-star has many finely folded lines that will need to be *creased with the back of a knife.*

1–3. Fold 2 diagonals in each of 4 squares. Fold one side according to the diagrams; crease carefully then open out these folds.

A little of the blue color was extracted from the tissue paper which was then tinted with red-violet on one segment corner. This made the center transverse slightly darker.

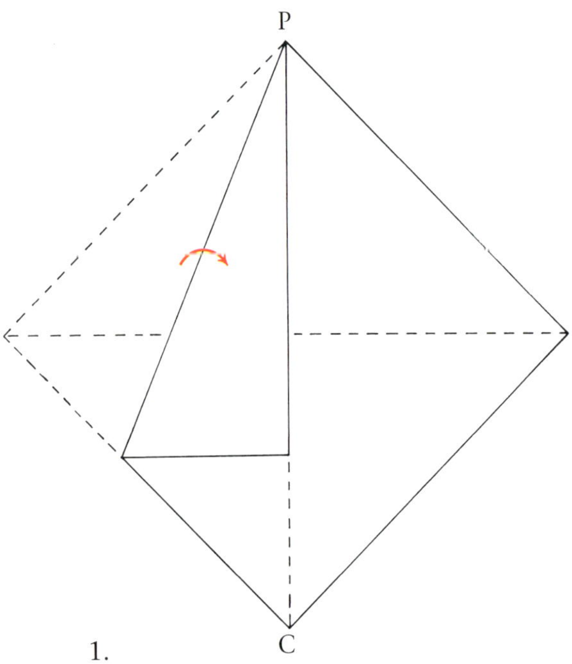

1.

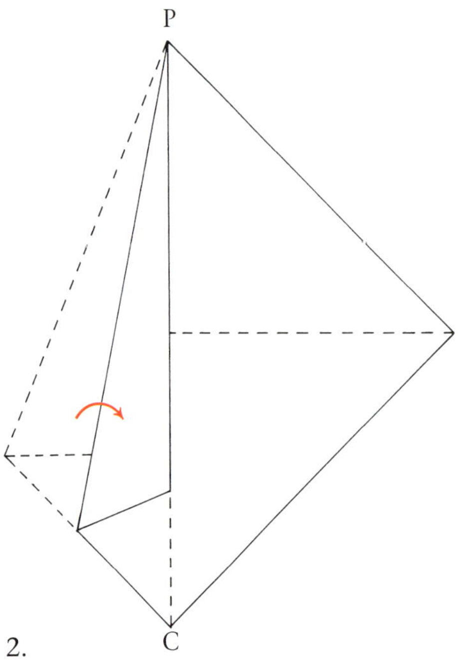

2.

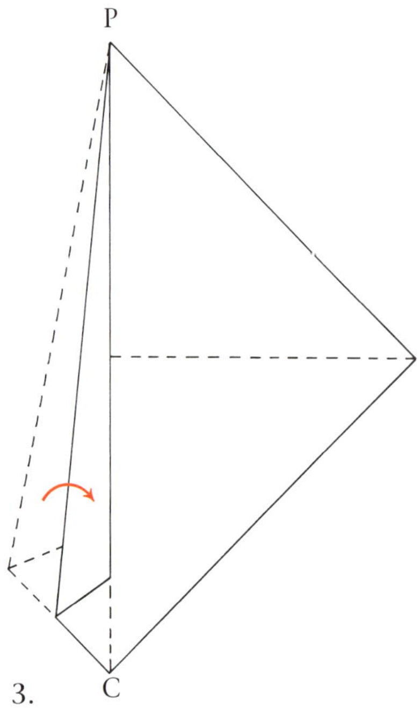

3.

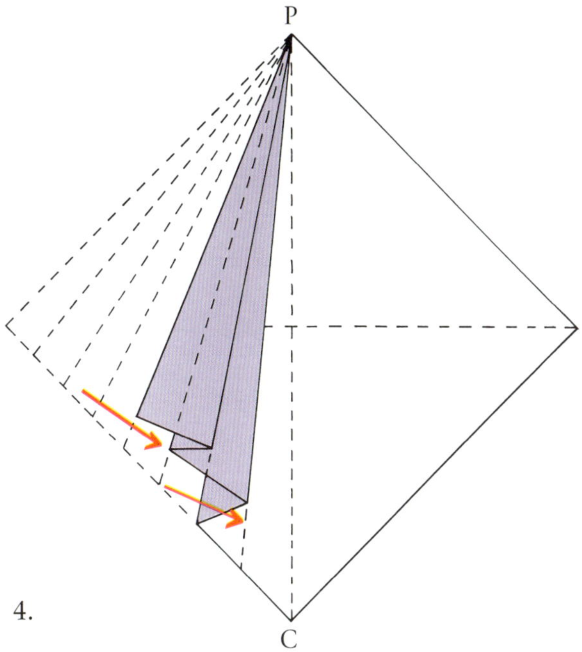

4.

4. Place folds on the support lines according to the diagram. This pleating falls into place naturally.

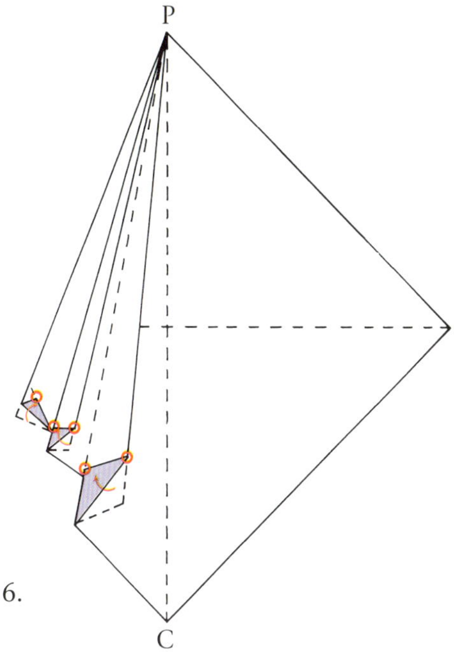

6.

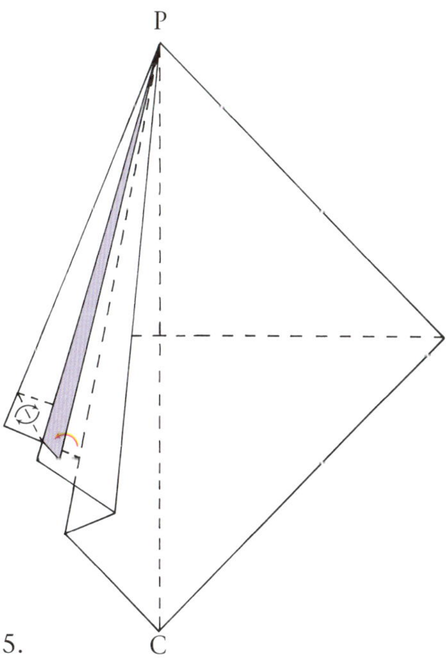

5.

5–6. Fold according to the diagrams and glue down the 3 corners. *Repeat the process for the other side of the segment.*

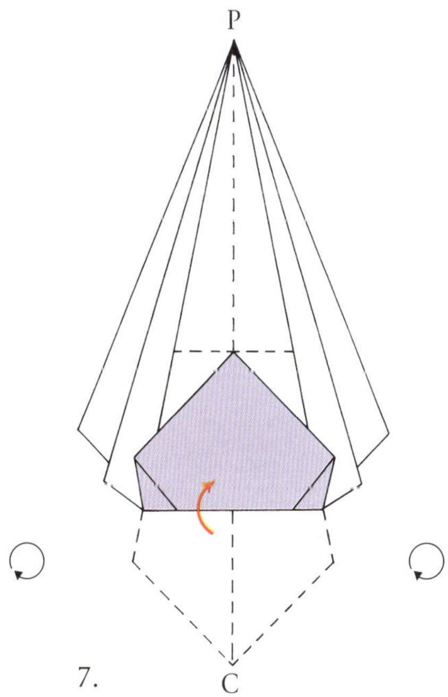

7.

7. Turn the piece over and fold (C) up to the midpoint. Turn the segment over again to the front side.

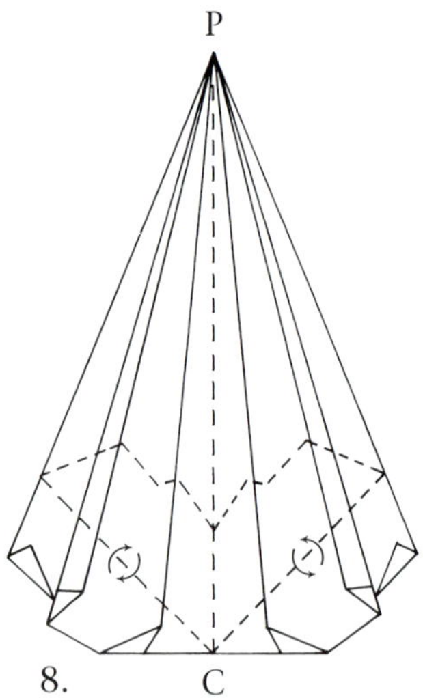

8.

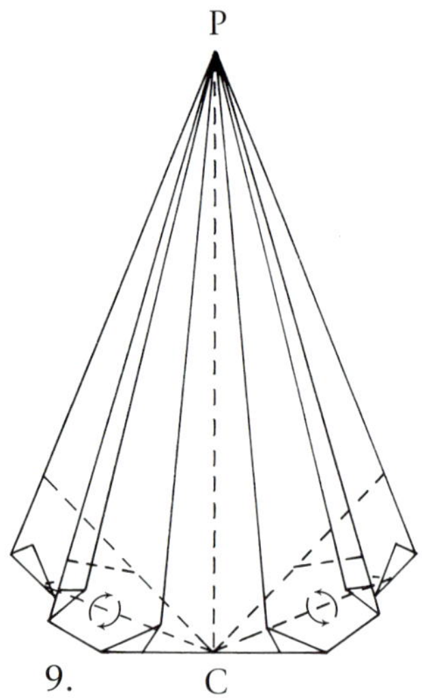

9.

8–9. Make support folds according to the diagrams.

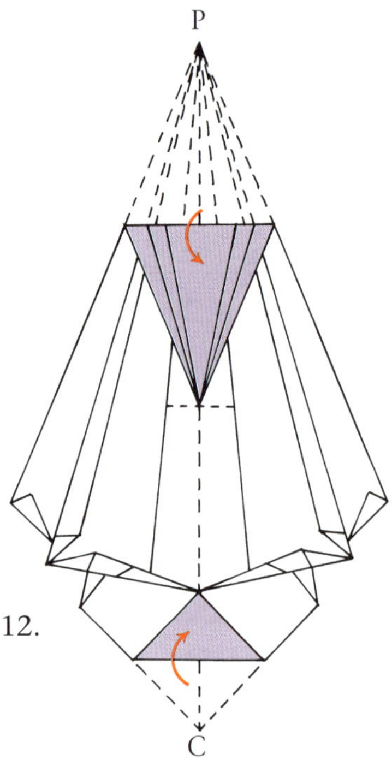

12.

12. Fold (P) and (C) according to the diagram.

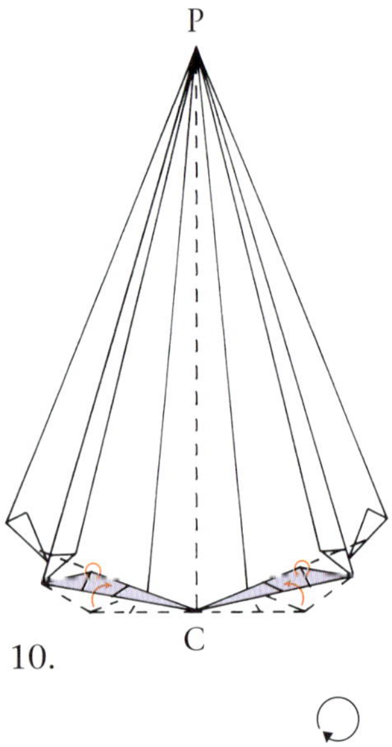

10.

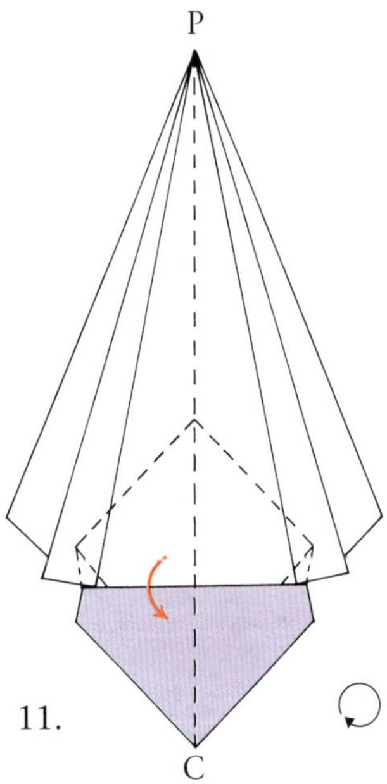

11.

10. Fold the lower edges up, in line with the outer base angle. Glue, *then turn the piece to the back side.*

11. Fold out the (C) section and *turn the piece back to the front side.*

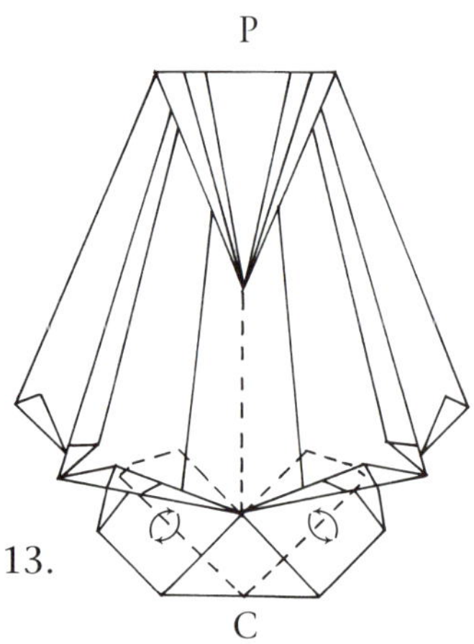

13.

13. Fold again the two support lines. Since the corners are thicker now, you don't need to crease the lines too tightly.

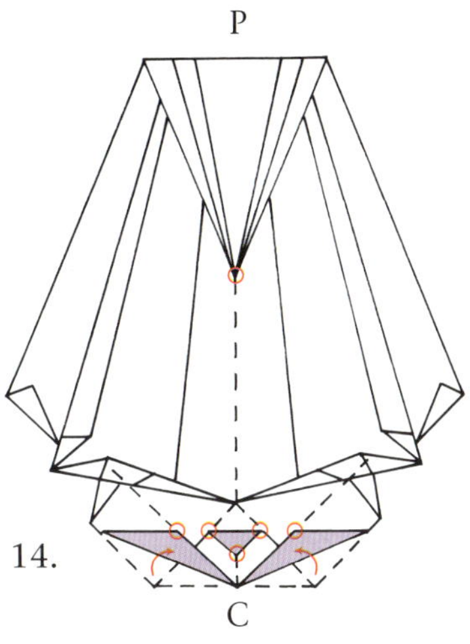

14. Fold up the base edges and glue to the fold line. Fold down the center triangle so that its upper edge is in line with the base edges to its right and left. Glue 6 indicated places.

The paper for the orange cross was not altered.

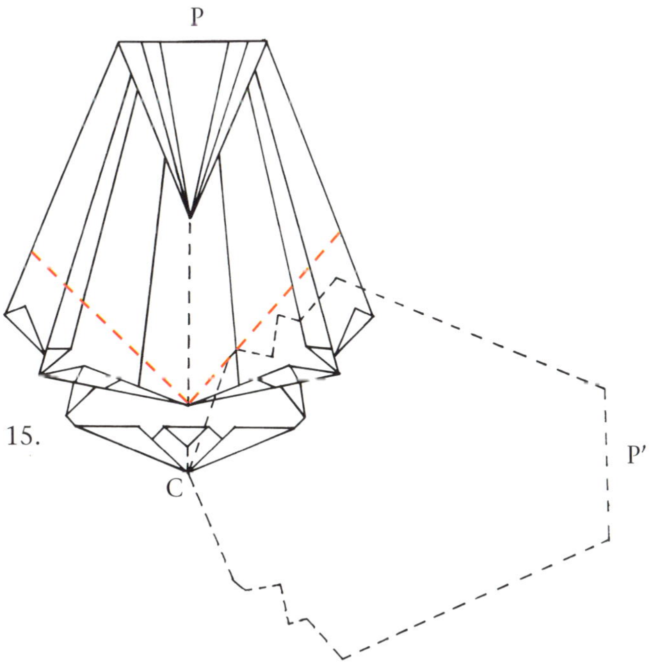

15. For assembly, the transverse fold line (red dotted line) serves as an orientation line. As indicated in the diagram, only the tiny left transverse edge of the next segment is glued to this line. Secure the structure on the back side of the cross with long glue lines. This will allow the beautiful, clear structure to come forth.

20. Cold Reflection **

figure with 6 rays
diameter:
35.5 cm (14") Cut 3
24.5 cm (9.6") Cut 4
17.5 cm (6.9") Cut 1

The unfolded rays of this transparency give the impression of a clear ice field beginning to melt on the window pane. Ice crystals form and dissolve in a moment.

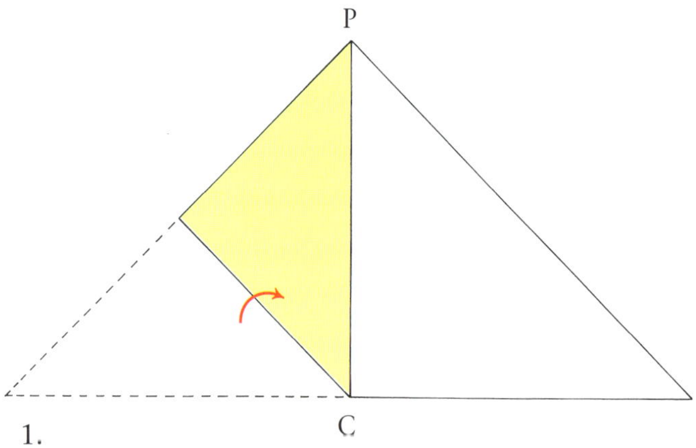

1.

1–2. Cut 3 squares in half to make 6 triangles. See triangular cuts, p. 10. Fold the midline of each triangle. Fold the left side of the triangle according to the diagrams.

On the facing page, the white paper was shaded with silver drops. For the little blue crystal, much of the color was removed from the paper.

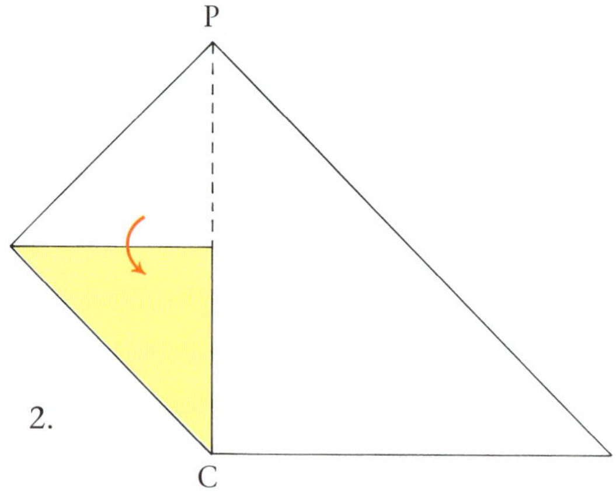

2.

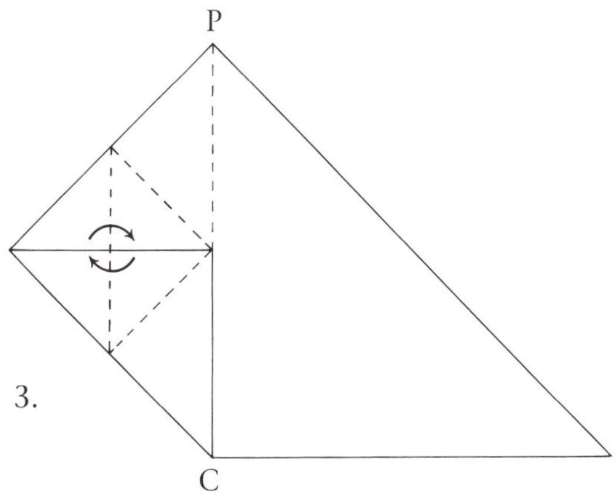

3.

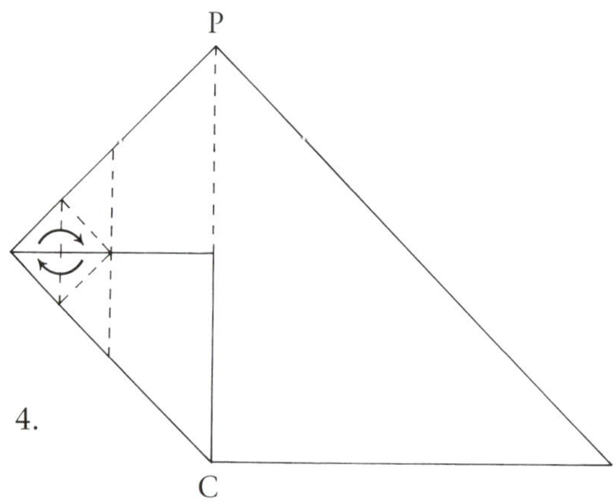

4.

3–4. Fold the corner to the midline and open again to create support lines.

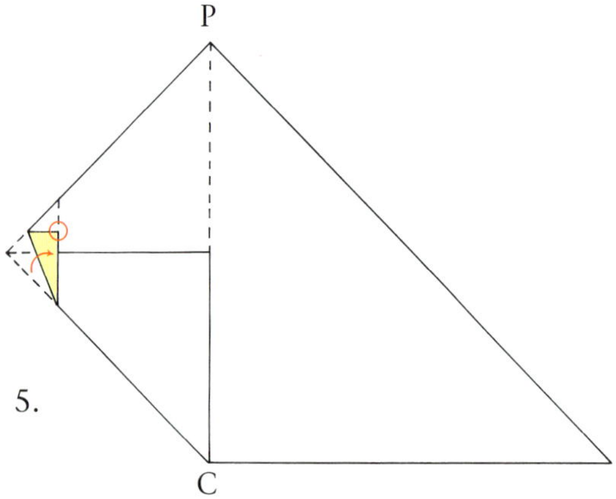

5.

5. Fold the corner to the bottom support line and glue in place.

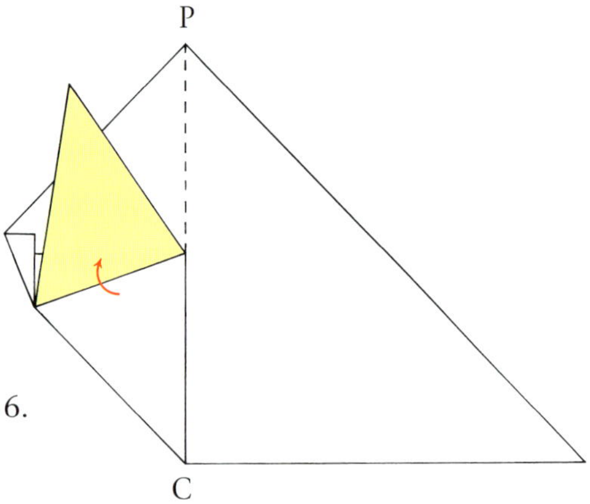

6.

6. Fold the loose corner back from the two support points until its folded edges touch the indicated border. *Repeat steps 1–6 for the right half.*

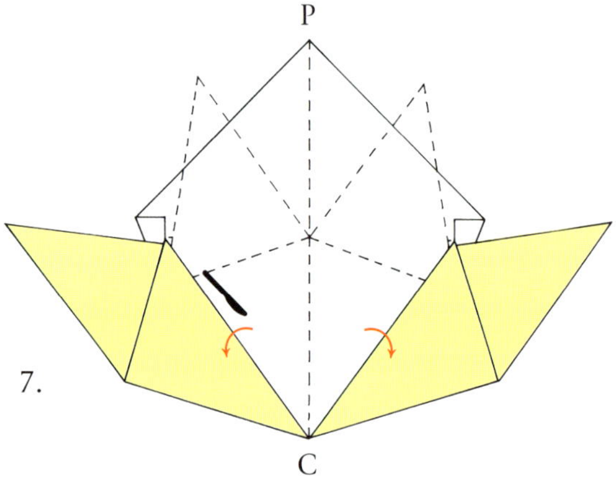

7.

7. Open the side wings outward so that the folded edges meet the fastened small triangles. Use the knife back to crease these folds, which must taper out exactly at the (C) point underneath.

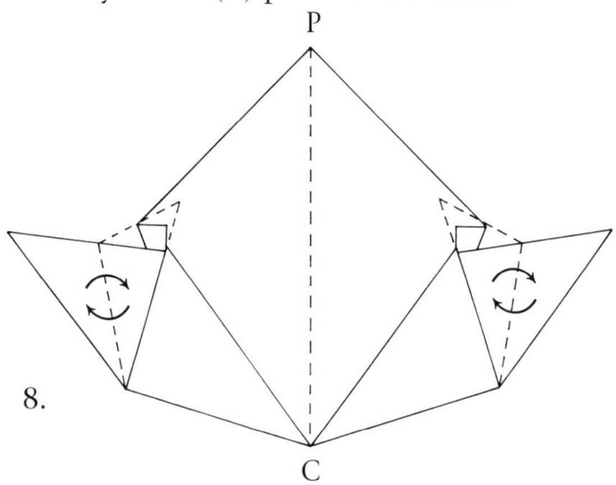

8.

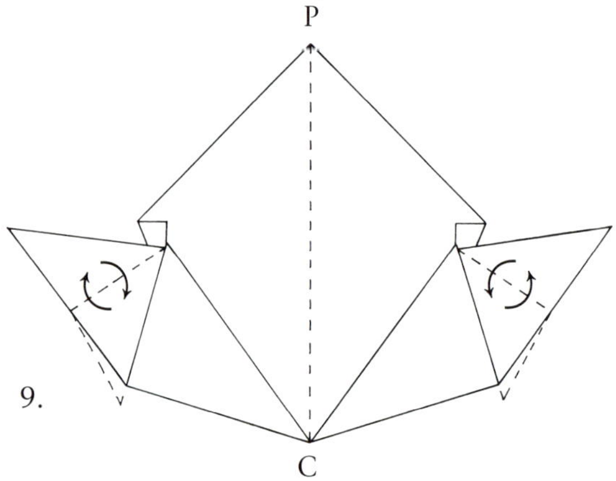

9.

8–9. Fold support lines in the two wing tips.

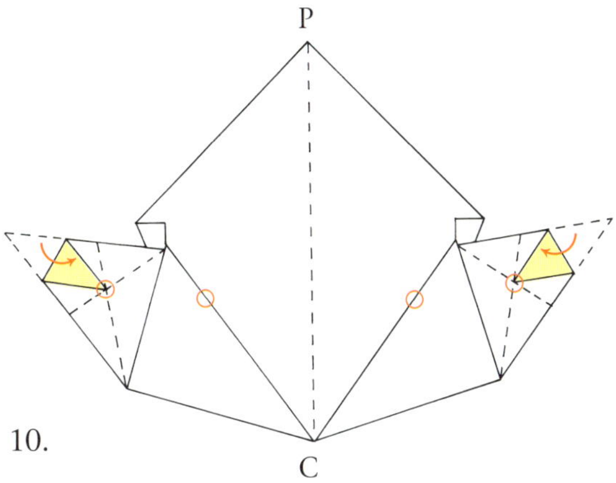

10.

10. Glue the tips and then the two spots on the transverse folds.

Assemble the 6 segments according to the template for a 6-rayed figure (see page 16). Note that the last folded corners appear to the right and left of a midline on each ray.

The light blue tissue paper was liberally sprinkled with white droplets.

21. Bouquet of Tulips *****

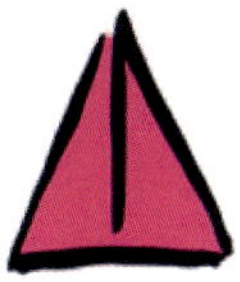

30 cm (11.8") high, Cut 3
21 cm (8.25") high, Cut 4

Another very interesting folding technique is used for this stylized bouquet of tulips. The leaves are folded in the same way as the petals are until the last step. The green stem is turned over and has additional folds. The elegant movement of the stem and leaves balances the heaviness of the blossoms. Leaf and blossom as metamorphosis of each other!

This strong pattern also looks very attractive in one solid color.

Some of the color was extracted from the paper for the large bouquet of tulips (left). Then the paper was lightly tinted with a warm orange tone.

For the petals, you will need 2 squares in any bright color; for the leaves, take 1 green square of the same size.

Fold each square twice, in order to obtain two diagonals. Then follow steps 1-3 from Tourmaline (p. 61). Open the folds to obtain support lines. Cut the three squares in triangles following the diagonals. You will have six triangles, of which you will use four. (See Triangular Cuts p. 10.)

Folding the petals and the leaves:

1.

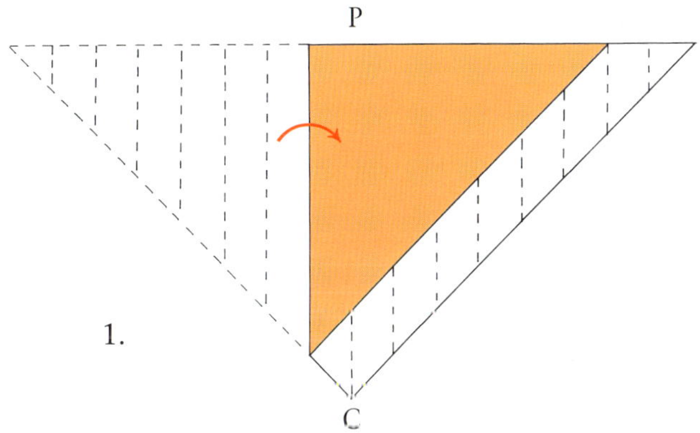

2.

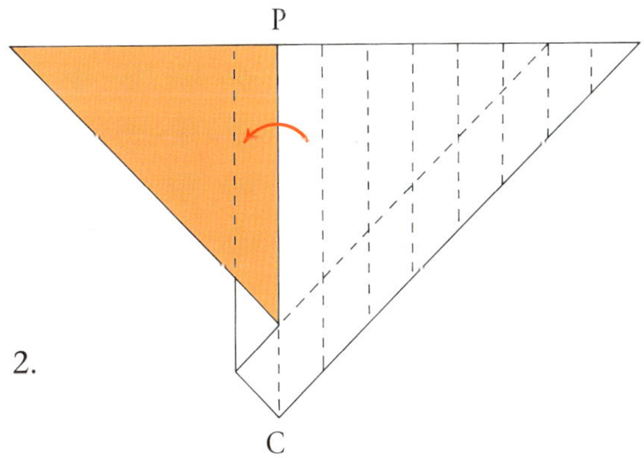

1–2. Fold the left side exactly, according to the diagrams. *Fold the right side in the same manner.*

3.

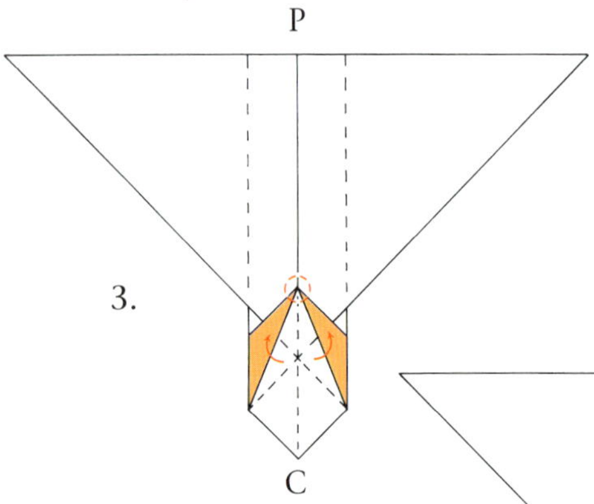

4.

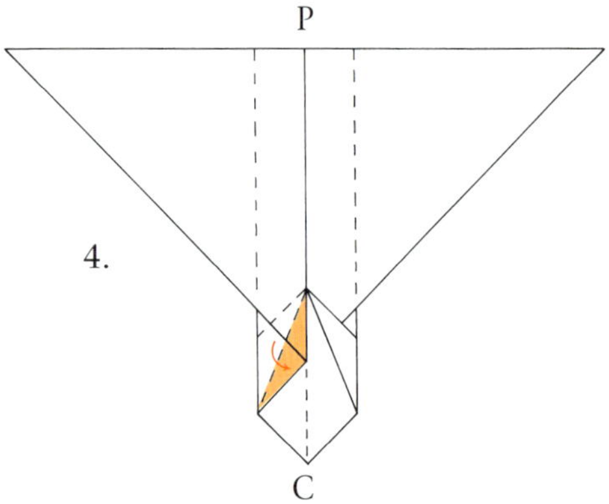

5.

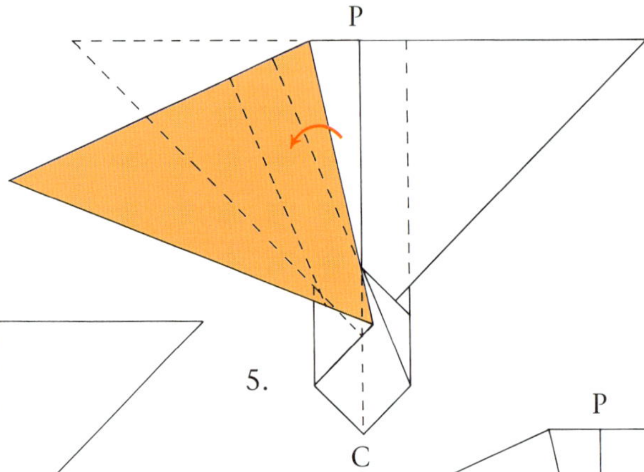

6.

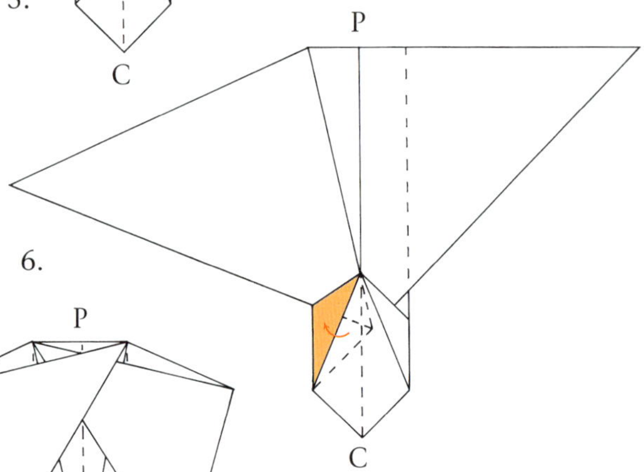

3. Open the middle of the center (C). From below, apply glue sparingly to attach folded corners to the midline.

4–6. Open out the lower left fold. Hold the glue point with your finger as you lower the left wing till the fold has completely opened flat near (P). Refold the lower left fold so that it lies flat in line with the new wing fold, then fold it up again over the bottom of the wing. *Repeat these steps for the right half of the figure.*

8.

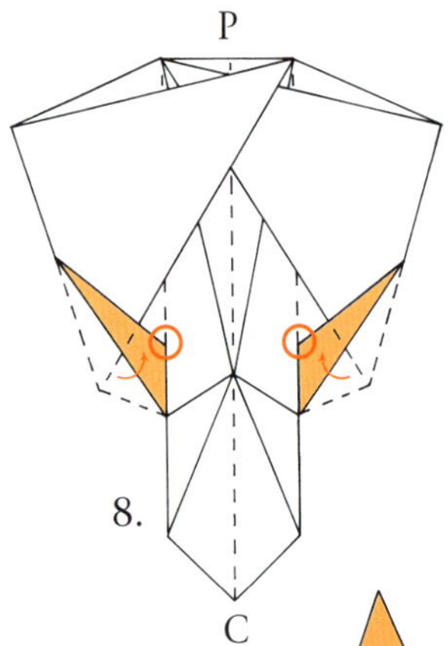

7.

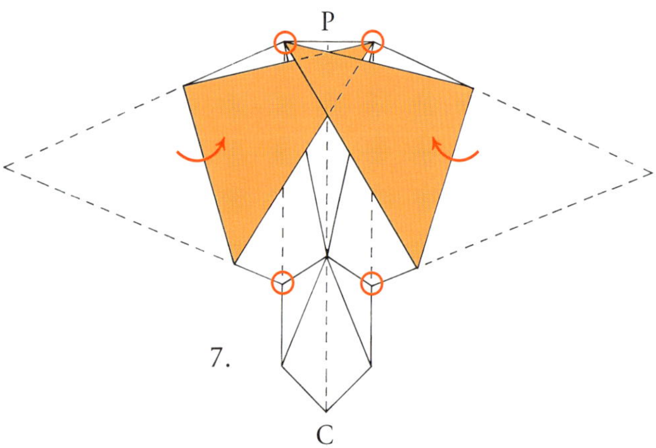

9.

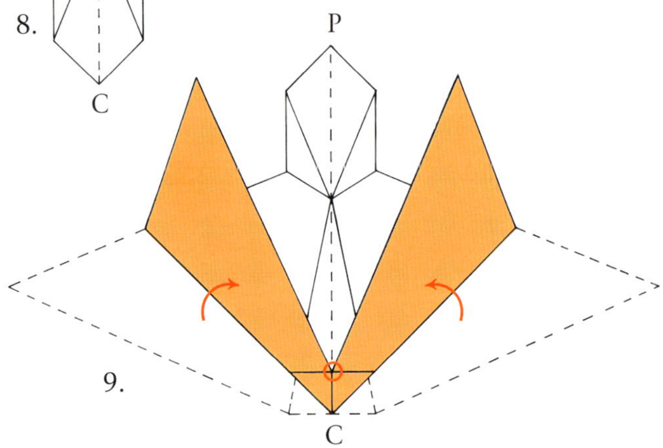

For petals only:
7–8. Fold and glue according to the diagrams.

For the stem and leaves only:
9. *Turn the green folded segment around so that the (C) point becomes (P) and vice versa.* Fold up both wings from the (C) point and glue in place.

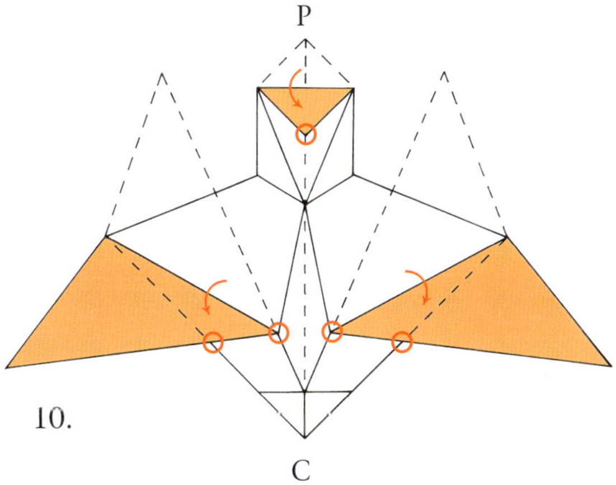

10.

10. Fold the wings back down, with the fold line beginning at the inner edge of the (C) area. Outer edges must be completely flat. Fold (P) down to the midline at the top edges of the side folds. Glue the 5 indicated places.

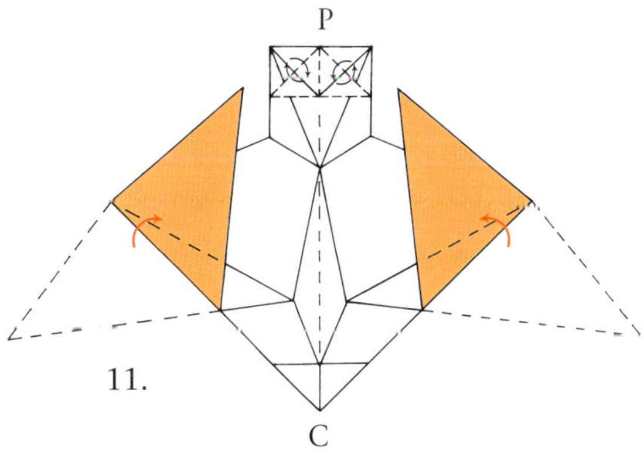

11.

11. Fold the corners at (P) to the midline and open again forming support lines. Fold the wings upward as indicated.

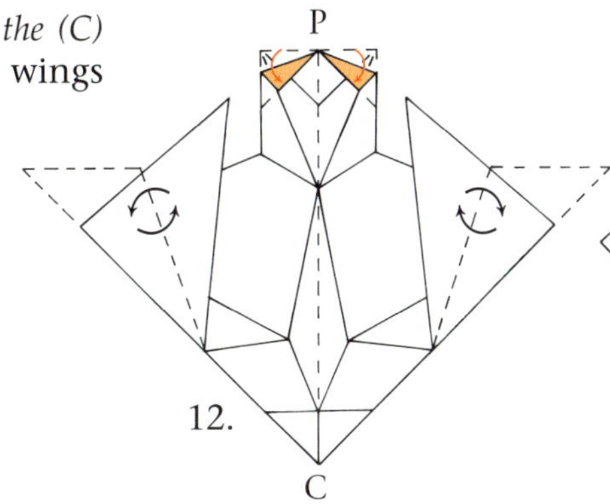

12.

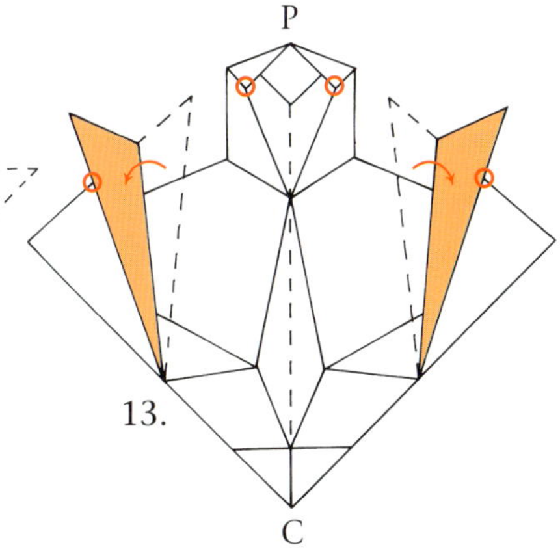

13.

12. Fold corners at (P) down to the support lines. Fold wings down to make another support line.

13. Fold wings to the support lines. Glue the 4 places indicated.

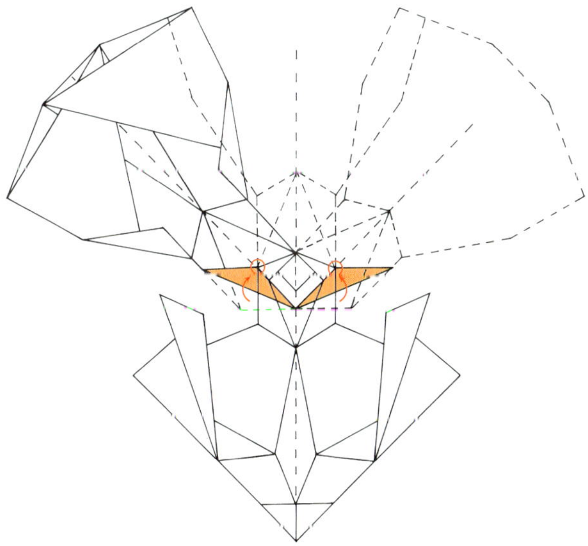

Assembly:
14. First assemble the 3 blossoms as for an 8-pointed star (see page 14). For the calyx, fold the lower corner of the right and left blossom up to its own midline and glue in place. Glue the petal construction to the green stem alligning the midlines of the stem and the central flower.

22. Sun Disk ****

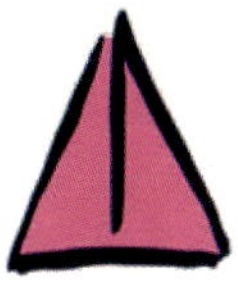

figure with 8 rays
diameter:
33.5 cm (13.2") Cut 3
24.5 cm (9.6") Cut 4
17.5 cm (6.9") Cut 1

The particular character of this eight-fold solar disc is achieved through the interplay of light stars, dark bundled rays and small decorative croppings around the inner rosette. You can clearly see the transformed tulip motif from the previous pattern.

Four square cuts are needed here, which you will prepare as for the beginning of Bouquet of Tulips (p. 79). Form the support lines accordingly, then divide your segments into eight triangles. Proceed to the end of step 6.

Once you have your eight segments, proceed with the following indications:

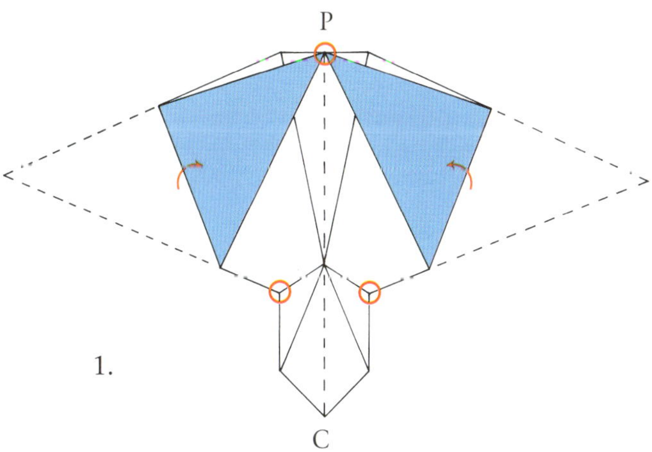

1.

1. Fold the side wings to the midline and glue the 3 places indicated.

2.

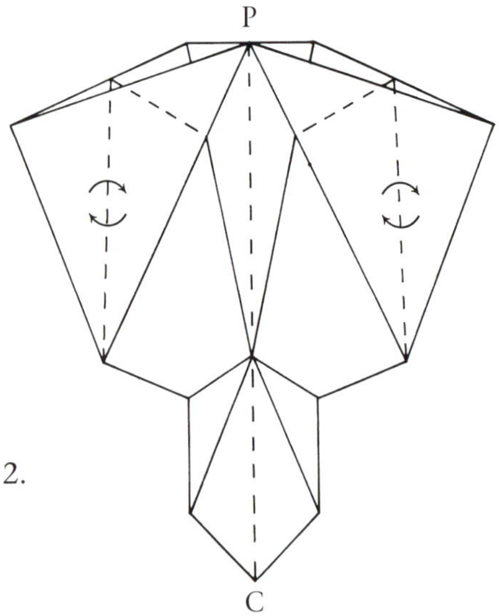

2. Fold the outer edges to the inner edges of the wings and open again, creating a support line.

3.

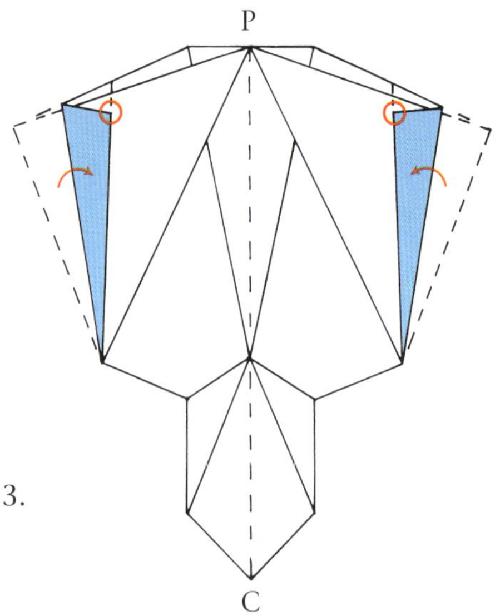

3. Fold the outer edges to these support lines and glue in place.

Assemble as for an 8-pointed star (see instructions on p. 14). The clarity of the inner rosette depends entirely on the exact positioning of the edges on the midlines.

23. *Star Dance* *

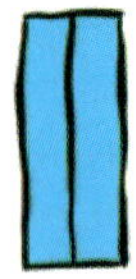

figure with 5 rays
diameter:
30 cm (11.8") Cut 7
20 cm (7.9") Cut 6

It seems as though this charming star wants to do a merry dance on the window pane. It is quick and easy to fold.

Some color was extracted from orange tissue paper before cutting for the larger five-pointed star. The yellow paper for the smaller star was treated the same way, then lightly tinted with orange watercolor.

Fold 5 rectangular pieces lengthwise to form a midline.

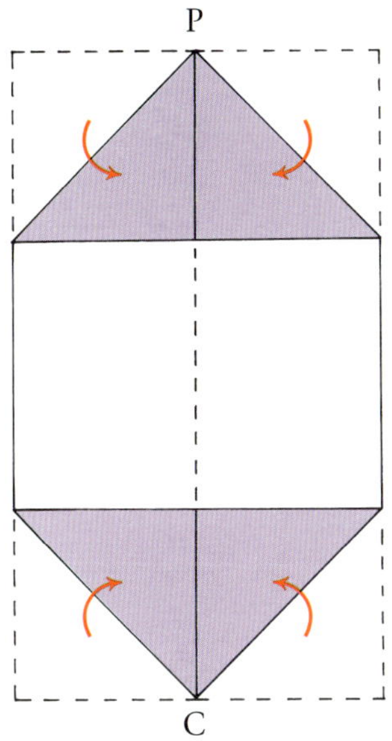

1.

1. Fold all four corners to the midline.

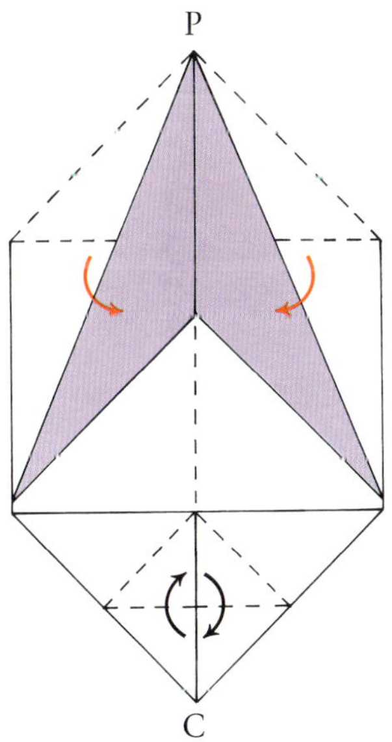

2.

2. Fold the upper corners at (P) down to the midline. Make a support line by folding the (C) point up to the midline and opening it again.

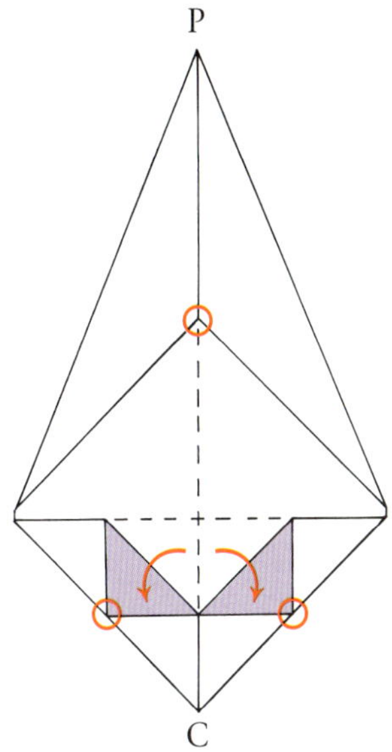

3.

3. Fold the loose corners at (C) out to the ends of the new support line. Glue the 3 indicated places.

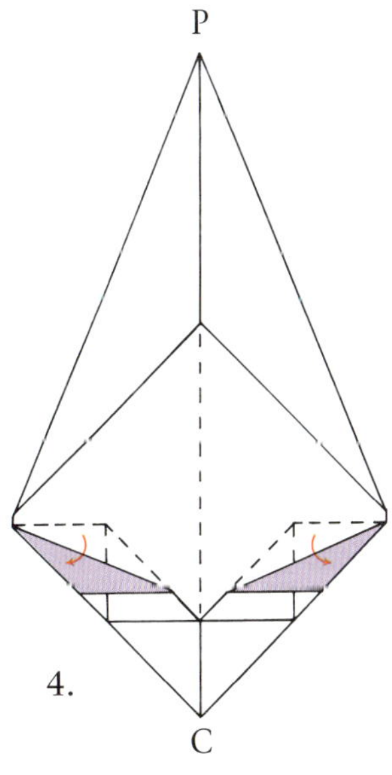

4.

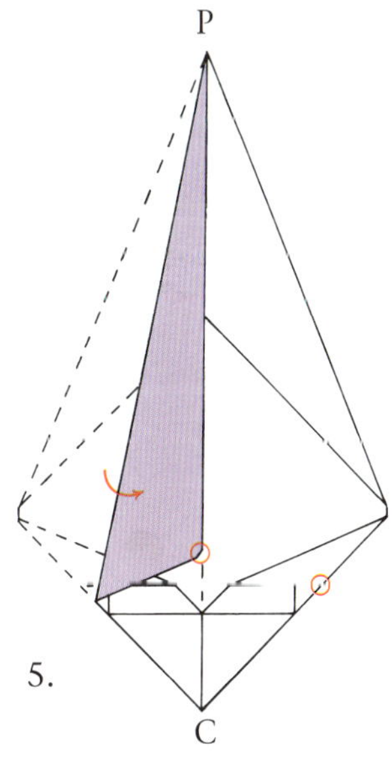

5.

4–5. Finish folding and gluing as indicated in the diagrams.

Assemble according to instructions for a 5-pointed star (see page 16).

24. Radiant Elegance **

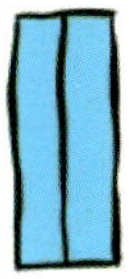

figure with 8 rays
diameter:
30 cm (11.8") Cut 7
20 cm (7.9") Cut 6

This elegant star reveals a beautiful play of light and shadow. Its finely chiseled inner core seems to radiate like a gem.

Take 8 rectangular cuts and follow *the entire procedure* of the previous transparency (Star Dance p. 85) up to step 5. This time though, you must fold both wings to the midline, *without applying glue points*.

At this point, the folding procedure is as follows:

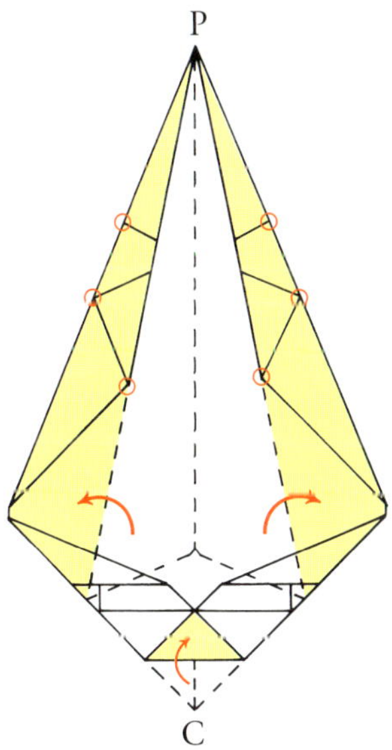

1.

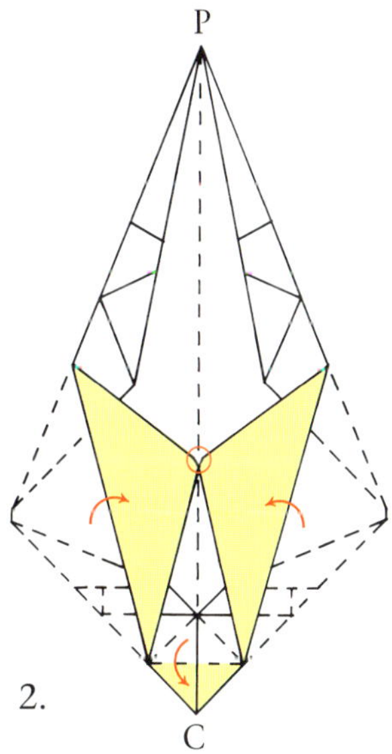

2.

1. Open the wings again and glue at the 6 places indicated. Temporarily fold the (C) point up as shown in the diagram.

2. Fold the side wings inward to the midline from the ends of the (C) fold line. Glue the wings and then open out the (C) fold. (If you are doing cut 6, for 7.9" (20 cm) diameter your segment is finished.)

< *The tissue paper for this purple star was enlivened with regularly placed large water drops.*

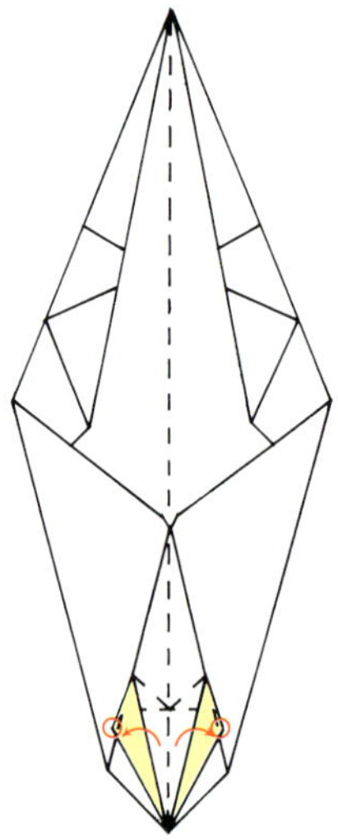

3.

For the larger format only:
3. You may add another fold at (C) to sharpen the center. Open the loose edges at (C) outward, slightly overlapping the edges of the wing fold. Glue in place.

Assemble according to instructions for an 8-pointed star (see page 14).

25. Multifoliate Rose *****

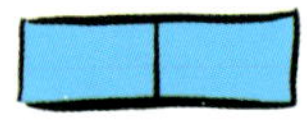

figure with 14 rays
diameter:
39.5 cm (15.5") Cut 9
28 cm (11") Cut 8

This exceptional flower is the crowning glory of the three-dimensional possibilities. This rose, with each segment's freely movable folds, wants to express what is in its heart. There is no scent, but when we see its soft fullness, it is easy to imagine a subtle fragrance.

Fold a midline parallel to the short sides of 14 rectangles.

The white tissue paper for the upper rose was sprinkled with drops of pink watercolor. >

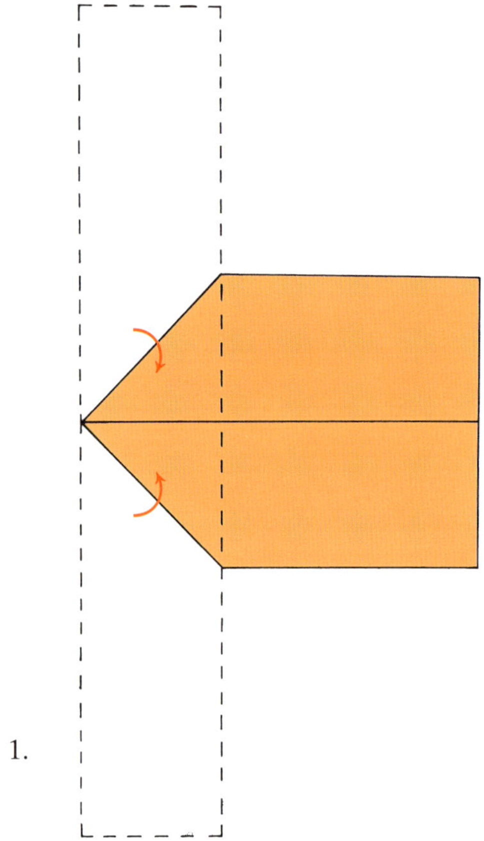

1. Fold the two halves together at the midline as shown in the diagram.

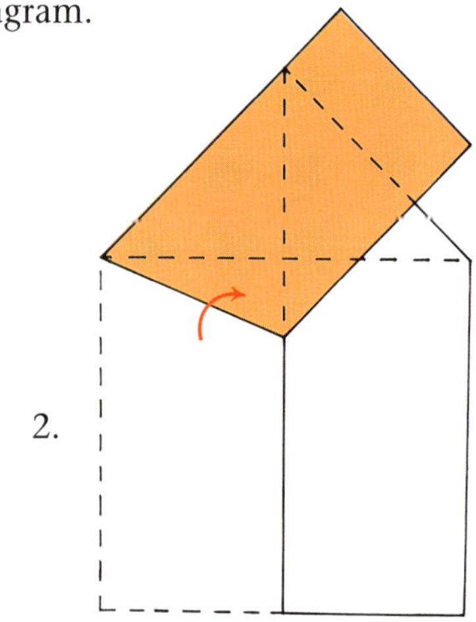

Preliminary folds:
2. Fold the left wing up and over the right half as shown.

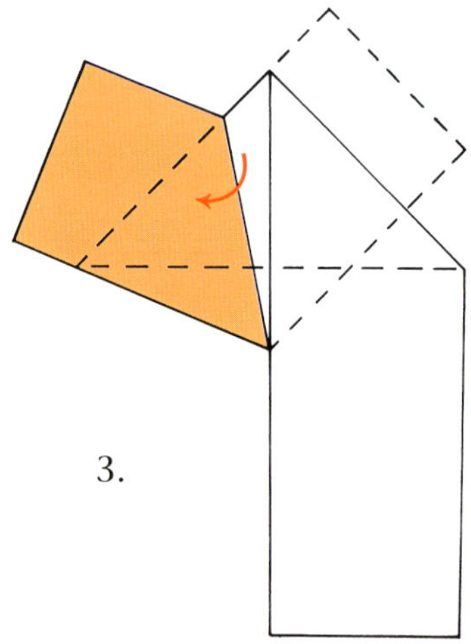

3. Fold this wing back alligning its edge with the fold below it. *Fold the right side to mirror the left following the same procedure. Now open up all the folds. You are now back at step 1 with all the necessary support lines.*

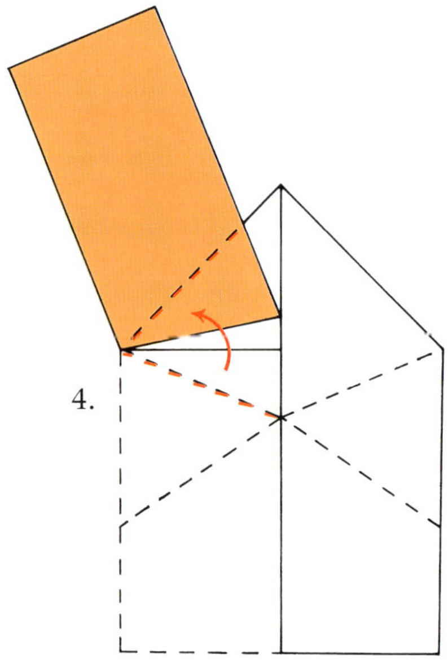

4. Allign the slanted support line of the left wing onto its upper edge.

5.

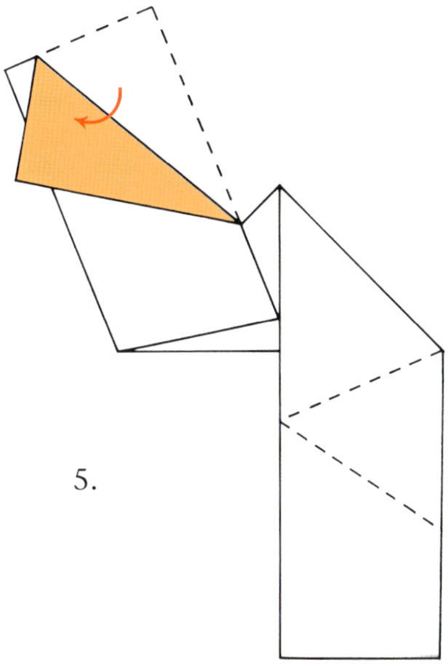

5. Fold down the right corner to the other support line. *Repeat steps 4 and 5 for the right side to mirror the left.*

6.

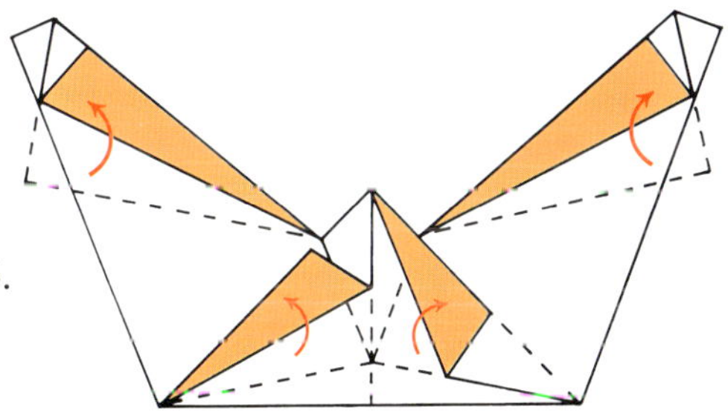

6. Make folds as indicated in the diagram.

7.

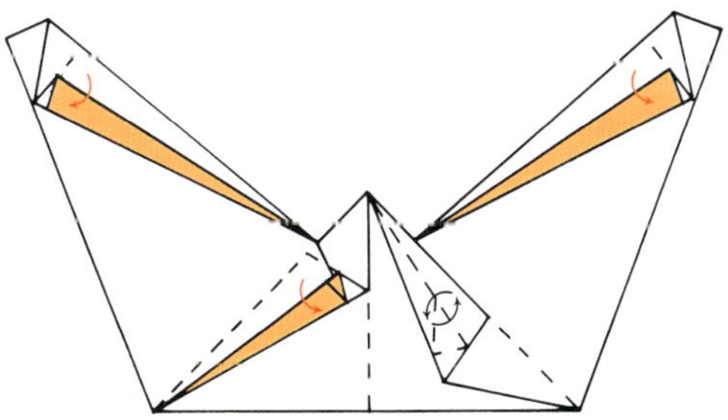

7. Continue according to the diagram. Note that the lower right fold is only made to create a support line for the assembly. *No glue is used in forming the segments.*

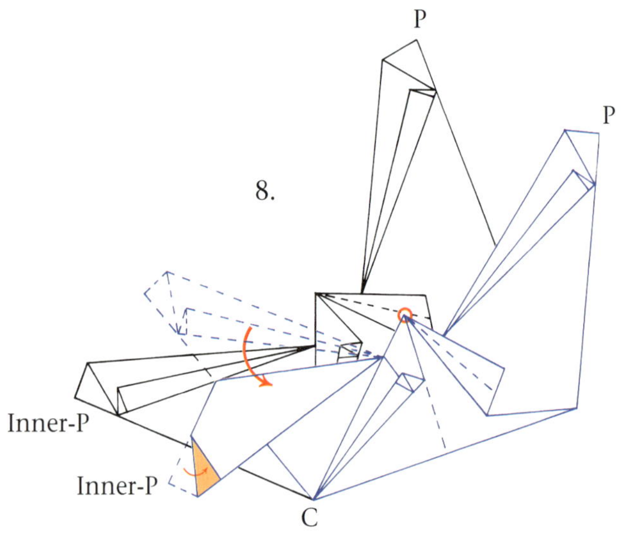

8. Assembly of the 14 segments.

The left base angle becomes the center (C).

The diagram shows the assembly of two finished segments.

Find the orientation point for the larger version at 5/32″ (2.5 mm) (for the smaller one, cut 8, at 3/32″ (1.5 mm)) off the last support line. Put a tiny spot of glue at this place so that you may easily correct for any slight irregularity.

To form the heart of the rose, fold every second left inner tip (inner P) to the inside back on the existing fold line. Then bend back the small angle. Carefully turn your transparency over so that you can fasten the middle rays on the back with long glue lines.

On the window, your Multifoliate Rose will unfold by itself.

For the tea rose, an orange sheet of paper was placed on a yellow one and some of the orange color was removed with a damp sponge before the paper was cut.

Making Magical Fairy-tale Puppets

Christel Dhom

In this book Christel Dhom presents new and imaginative possibilities in working with "Fairy's wool," or unspun wool. She gives special emphasis to the mobiles, or hanging dolls, that represent fairy-tale characters. The dolls can also be made as toys to be played with or as standing puppets rather than as mobiles.

ISBN 0-945803-58-3

72 pages

RUDOLF STEINER COLLEGE PRESS

Making Fairy-tale Wool Animals

Angelika Wolk-Gerche

Fairy-tale wool—high quality carded unspun fiber, in natural colors or plant dyed—has long been used in Waldorf kindergartens. Teachers have devised many ways of creating figures for decoration, for play, or for acting out songs, poems, and fairy tales. This book gives clear instructions for parent or teacher, advanced craftperson or beginner. Many projects can also be done by children.

ISBN 0-945803-60-5
80 pages

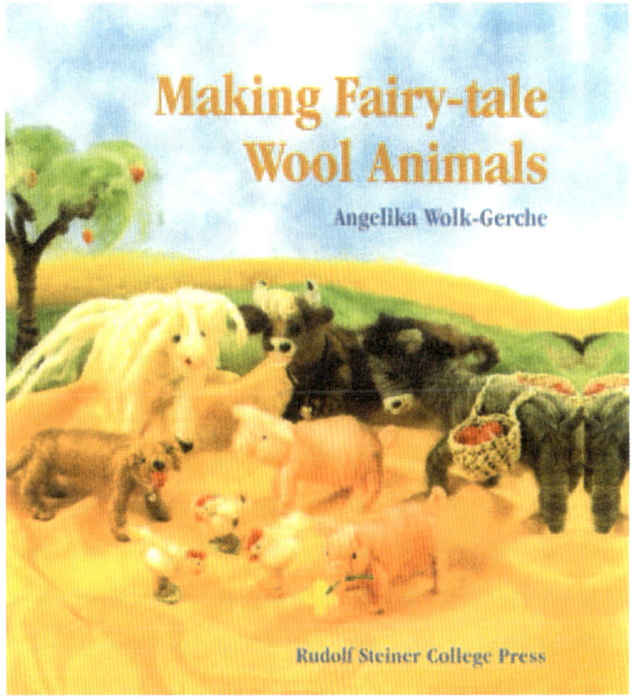

RUDOLF STEINER COLLEGE PRESS